MICHELE BARBI'S
LIFE OF DANTE

MICHELE BARBI'S LIFE OF DANTE

Translated and Edited by
PAUL G. RUGGIERS

UNIVERSITY OF CALIFORNIA PRESS
Berkeley and Los Angeles: MCMLXVI

UNIVERSITY OF CALIFORNIA PRESS
Berkeley and Los Angeles, California

CAMBRIDGE UNIVERSITY PRESS
London, England

Copyright, 1954
By The Regents of the University of California

Third printing, 1966
(First Paper-bound Edition, Second Printing)

Dante: Vita, opere e fortuna first published
in Florence by G. C. Sansoni, 1933
Library of Congress Catalog Card Number: 54-6466

Designed by Adrian Wilson

Translator's Preface

Although there are many useful books that describe Dante's development as a social being, a poet, and a citizen against the background of his times, none of them seem to me to surpass the late Michele Barbi's account for compactness, unity, and scholarly combination of the best of the early commentators with the findings of modern research.

Michele Barbi's life came to an end in 1941 when he was seventy-four years old; it had been a life of extraordinary productivity and assiduous devotion to Italian literature and philology, with special emphasis upon Dante. The present work first appeared in the *Enciclopedia Italiana* in 1931 and was later published in book form as *Dante: Vita, opere e fortuna* in Florence in 1933. Barbi's indefatigable and painstaking work on the texts of the *Vita Nuova,* the Canzoniere, and the *Divina Commedia,* his interest in problems relating to Dante's life and work, his positions as general editor of the Italian edition of Dante's works, which appeared in 1921, as director of the *Bolletino della Società Dantesca Italiana* from 1893 to 1905, and founder of *Studi Danteschi* (1920), qualified him preëminently to be Dante's most recent, authoritative Italian biographer.

It cannot be denied that Dante's genius demands constant elucidation. If a reason was needed for making known another life of Dante, as Barbi has done, it would be found in the provocative complexity of Dante's own personality as it is expressed in his work. A biography which enables us to consider as a whole the life of one whom T. S. Eliot calls "the most universal of poets in the modern languages" serves a real purpose and satisfies a real need. For Dante, like all great poets, supplies in small compass an encyclopedia of the learning of his time. The greater the poet, the greater the need for describing his greatness, his importance linguistically, politically, theologically, historically, and poetically. All this Barbi has done for us.

It is especially valuable that English-speaking readers should have made available to them a life of Dante by a writer who was himself an Italian and whose point of view is so entirely sympathetic with the greatest of Italian poets. It is in this mixture of natural sympathy for Dante's aims with sober judgment and scholarly care that the value of Barbi's biography resides.

Dante's works themselves form a kind of biography. The *Vita Nuova,* the *Convivio,* the *De Vulgari Eloquentia,* the Canzoniere, the *Epistles,* the *Eclogues,* and the *Commedia* are all memorable in one way or another for poignant passages in which Dante records his anxieties, his frustrations, and his hopes, together with names of places and persons he has known. Barbi himself has given tacit evidence of this. The reader who has familiarized himself with Dante will find many reminiscences of the poet's own language in that of Barbi. For this reason I have taken few liberties with the translation. Barbi's formal, scholarly Italian I have rendered as closely as possible, breaking sentences only when their great length would make them involved and confusing in translation. By so doing I have hopes that the reader may feel something of the harmony that existed between the biographer and his subject.

I gratefully acknowledge a great debt to Professor Elio Gianturco, of the University of Pennsylvania, for his many suggestions for improving the style and accuracy of the text.

P. G. R.

Contents

PART I: THE LIFE OF DANTE ALIGHIERI

Social Status and Early Education	3
Experiments in Art and Scholarship	5
Domestic Life and Public Office	9
The Early Years of Exile	16
The Origin of the Great Poem	21
The Descent of Henry VII	23
The Last Years	26

PART II: THE MINOR WORKS

The Minor Works and the "Trilogy"	33
The *Vita Nuova*	35
The Minor Poems	39
The *Convivio*	43
De Vulgari Eloquentia	50
The *Epistles*	52
De Monarchia	56
The *Eclogues*	64
Quaestio de aqua et terra	65

PART III: THE DIVINE COMEDY

Genesis and Composition	69
Inferno	73
Purgatorio	76
Paradiso	79

PART III: THE DIVINE COMEDY (*continued*)

The Poetic Unity of the *Commedia*	83
Dante's World View	88
Present and Past in Dante's Vision	92
Dante in His Poem	97
Dante's Genius	100

PART IV: THE REPUTATION AND STUDY OF DANTE   109

TRANSLATOR'S NOTES   117

BIBLIOGRAPHICAL NOTE   125

Part I
The Life of Dante Alighieri

Social Status and Early Education

Dante was born in Florence, May, 1265. His family, it was thought, was descended from the "noble seed of the Roman founders" of the city.* It could be called noble also by virtue of titles and dignities which it later earned,† although it was subsequently reduced to modest circumstances. His great-great-grandfather Cacciaguida‡ had been knighted by Emperor Conrad III, and had died, according to Dante's own testimony, during the Second Crusade in the Holy Land; Cacciaguida was probably related to the Elisei, and in fact, his house was situated near the Old Market where that family dwelt.§ His descendants, however, removed to the district of San Martino, and here Dante was born, the son of Alighiero di Bellincione d'Alighiero. The family was Guelph, as were most of the city's lesser nobility and artisans, in opposition to the feudal aristocracy of the Ghibelline party.[1] This aristocracy, under the protection of the Empire, managed to hold the upper hand in the commune. Although Dante proclaims through the mouth of Farinata degli Uberti** that his ancestors had been fiercely hostile to the Ghibellines, at whose hands they twice suffered exile, their names never appear in any account of those struggles, and there is but meager docu-

---
* *Inf.*, XV, 73–78.
† *Par.*, XVI, 1–9.
‡ *Par.*, XV, 130–148.
§ *Par.*, XVI, 40–42.
** *Inf.*, X, 46.

mentary evidence of damages suffered by one of them in his own house. Despite the family's modest social standing (one sister married a public crier of the commune; another, Tana, a moneylender), Dante was able to pursue his studies and live the life of a gentleman. In 1289 he served the commune as a mounted soldier at Campaldino with the cavalry, among the front-line soldiers. He formed fast friendships with such proud aristocrats as Guido Cavalcanti; his father, before his death (1283?), arranged for his marriage to a gentlewoman of the Donati family, but of a distant branch whose power had passed into decline.

It has been claimed that Dante spent a great part of his adolescence as a Franciscan novice in the convent of Santa Croce, but there are too many indications that he led another kind of life which he anticipated and for which he was destined by his parents. We cannot exclude the possibility that he frequented the Franciscan lower schools, and later he attended their schools of philosophy. The study of rhetoric, which included both public speaking and letter writing in Latin (*ars dictaminis*), was pursued not only by judges and notaries, but also by those ambitious to become influential citizens; this subject seems to have been taught him by Brunetto Latini, who first set the Florentines to "governing the commonwealth according to sound policy." From him Dante avows that he learned "how a man becomes eternal."* There is evidence that he went to Bologna during his youth. If he was there for study, he probably attended the schools of rhetoric, much renowned at the time, rather than the schools of law. The influence of this formal study and his love for the Latin classics persisted throughout his life.

* *Inf.*, XV, 85.

Experiments in Art and Scholarship

While still a young man he learned by himself the art of "discoursing in rhyme,"* and thus very soon was able to make the acquaintance of the most famous troubadours of the city, asking questions of them or answering theirs, and circulating his love poetry, as was then the fashion. For many, this versifying was a mere embellishment, an extra accomplishment. For Dante, little by little, it became a serious occupation through his love of art, learning, and genuine love courtship, especially after he had formed a friendship with Guido Cavalcanti. Together they began to distinguish their own skill and art, as well as Lapo Gianni's, from that of Guittone, which seemed uncouth to them, and from that of other "coarse" writers who composed their rhymes carelessly; they greatly refined their own ideas about the nature and the effects of love on the interior perfection of man. Guido, given to subtleties of thought, cared more for natural philosophy than Dante did. Dante, being of a more artistic nature, preferred the study of the Latin poets, particularly Virgil, who became so much his teacher and his special author that later he acknowledged Virgil as the source of the "beautiful style" that made him famous.† From the beginning he must have felt time and again the influence of Guido's longer experience, but very soon his own poetic temperament, his classical studies, and the example of Guido Guinizelli* constrained him to bring about that innovation in vernacular poetry which he makes Bonagiunta Orbicciani praise in the *Purgatorio*.‡ His fame as an outstanding poet soon grew and spread. Thus in the leisure which cavalry expeditions and other military

---
* *Vita Nuova*, III, 9.
† *Inf.*, I, 82–87.
‡ *Pur.*, XXIV, 49–62.

duties' and the management of personal affairs left a man of his circumstances, he was able to find a noble occupation calculated to engage powerfully his self-esteem.

The grace and beauty of a Florentine gentlewoman made a deep impression upon his feelings. He called her by the full name Beatrice, to indicate that she brought happiness to all who looked upon her. (All the evidence shows that she was Bice, daughter of Folco Portinari, and, later, the wife of Simone dei Bardi.) Some fond remembrance of her, connected with his earliest youth, the conventional use to which these love affairs were then put in poetry and his own melancholy musings, coupled with a certain sweet modesty in the gentle girl which made her seem still more loftily virtuous,—all this gradually persuaded him that she must be, and indeed was, the guide of his thoughts and emotions toward that ideal perfection which is the goal of every noble mind. Hence, his poems no longer elicit the lamentations, customary with other poets, about the cruelty of the lady, no longer frequent demands for pity. Instead, we find her exalted as a miracle of courtesy and virtue, as a creature sent to earth by God not only for the welfare of her faithful lover, but for all those who might be disposed by nature to appreciate her noble qualities. Together with such an exaltation of the woman there is the fear that such a being could not be destined to remain long in this earthly life.

In the midst of these vague and anxious fancies, death actually came; first the death of Beatrice's father, and then her own on June 8, 1290. The poet's grief gave way to an intense contemplation of her in the glory of heaven. Soon, however, another gentlewoman, impelled by pity and apparently lamenting with him the loss of Beatrice, succeeded, sometime after the first anniversary of her death, in kindling love in him once more; but shortly thereafter the memory of Beatrice again triumphantly asserted itself, leaving in him remorseful qualms over having been faithless to the woman whom his eyes and heart should never have betrayed. It was in this feeling of renewed fidelity and grief that there arose in him the resolve to celebrate the virtue of Beatrice with greater solemnity by bringing together the scattered poems he had written in praise of her, and by explaining the true meaning and the occasion for each. Out of this plan evolved the little volume (*ca.* 1292–1293) which was, in its completed form, an innovation full of charm, even though it was made up of things already known and composed, for the most part, according to current convention. He called it the *Vita Nuova,* as if to mark the end of a period of preparation and the beginning of more significant things.

In the meantime his love of study had grown stronger. Boethius and Cicero* had opened wider horizons before his eyes. As a result of the diffusion of Aristotle's physical and metaphysical works, the speculative impulse revived; and the need for harmonizing the thought of this "teacher of human reason" with the truth of the Faith made itself felt. The rise of so many schools and universities, sponsored by the new religious orders, which drew even the laity toward philosophic speculation, attracted the poet, who was by now a grown man, to become a frequent visitor at the "schools of the religious and the disputations of the philosophers."† In the second half of the thirteenth century, the Dominican convent of Santa Maria Novella had a *studium solemne;* and from 1295 on, when the Roman province was reorganized, a *studium generale.* In Florence at that period there were eminent teachers among the Franciscans of Santa Croce; one of them, from 1287 to 1289, was Pietro Giovanni Olivi; and the schools of

---
* *Conv.*, II, xii, 2–5.
† *Ibid.*, II, xii, 7.

the Augustinians of Santo Spirito also formed an active intellectual center. According to Dante's own testimony, shortly after the year 1290 he applied his labors to philosophy with such zeal that "in a short time, perhaps thirty months," he began "to be so keenly aware of her sweetness that the love of her drove away and destroyed every other thought." Not more than two or three years had elapsed when, "having overtaxed his eyes with too much reading," he felt his visual powers to be so weakened that "the stars appeared to him to be shadowed by some white mist."*

Reflections of this passionate study were to be perceived in his poetry, since he now set himself the task not only of glorifying philosophy as the mistress of his mind, but also of handling subjects of moral philosophy, like nobility and genuine love courtship, in artistically wrought *canzoni*.

But not even for reasons of study would he abandon the "sweet discoursing of love" dedicated to living gentlewomen. Love remained for him the source of every noble action and every high purpose. The mark of the true gentleman, besides courage or valor, was courtesy, understood in the social sense of beautiful manners and therefore as "conversing with ladies in gallant fashion," paying poetic homage to beauty as the source of lofty enterprises and incitement to them. Moreover, the feeling and need for art in a temperament like Dante's were developing on independent lines. To his increasingly conscious admiration for the Latin poets he added a wider study of the poetry of the chief Provençal troubadours, and the desire to enter into competition with them led him to compose things new and untried. The results were, if nothing else, experiments in art which tested and strengthened his poetic talent for greater things in the future. One of these experiments is thought to be *Il Fiore*, a free paraphrase of

---

* *Conv.*, II, xii, 7; III, ix, 15.

the *Roman de la Rose* in 232 sonnets, done with uncommon skill and boldness; but the more we seek Dante's "touch" in this work, the less surely is it to be found there.

Domestic Life and Public Office

We need not, however, imagine the poet as entirely absorbed in his studies and poetic experiments. Life itself was a pressing reality. Furthermore, his was not a mind that could become engrossed in a purely intellectual world, indifferent to the relationship which art and knowledge bear to life.

In Florence a great social change was occurring. The intense development of crafts and trade, the influx of new people from the country, attracted by the rewards of monetary and political success, had more and more curtailed the power and privileges of the old noble families that had never been concerned with industry and commerce. On the one hand, money had brought with it arrogance and partisanship; on the other, extreme poverty had spawned wretchedness and desolation. Dante's father had been able to preserve and perhaps increase the family's small patrimony, if not precisely in the capacity of a moneylender, certainly in some kind of business. His son did not follow in his steps, nor did Dante's brother Francesco, who kept himself at a safe distance from study; Francesco seems to have been nothing more than a small property owner. Like all the lesser nobility who lived on income from landed property, our poet, too, soon felt the pinch of need; there is evidence in loan records that he and his brother ran into debt during the last years of the thirteenth century. From the poet's marriage with Gemma di Manetto Donati[ii] which was arranged in 1277, but effected we know not when, were born several children: Iacopo, Pietro, and Antonia (to be identified probably with a sister Beatrice who took the veil in the nunnery of Santo Stefano degli Olivi at Ravenna). A certain "Iohannes filius Dantis Alagherii de Florentia," who appears as a witness in a law suit on October 21, 1308, at Lucca, may be another son.

Dante and his brother, the latter himself married to a woman of his station, were obliged to live solely on the income from their properties and on the small profit to be derived from pasturing cattle on a sharing basis. This situation imposed restrictions and brought on straitened circumstances whenever special occasions demanded great expenditures either to uphold the dignity of the family or perhaps to improve its station. And indeed, in view of the breadth of Dante's talents and his aptitude and longing for the life of a gentleman in a city famed for her courtesy, such special times and occasions are not difficult to imagine. We see a hint of one such in the words uttered by Charles Martel in *Paradiso:**

> Much didst thou love me, and with good cause:
> Had I remained below, I would have shown thee
> Much more of my love than the leaves.

The Angevin prince, having come to Tuscany during February and March of 1294 to meet his father, who was returning from Provence, was much feted in Siena and Florence by Florentine knights placed under his orders by the commune. Among them must have been Dante who, it seems, received from the young prince such signs of affection as to arouse in him the most flattering hopes.'

But meanwhile the more Dante cherished his ideas of courtesy and valor, which made social life cheerful and virtuous, the more his city turned toward a materialist view of existence and became embroiled in a merciless internal battle as her

---

* *Par.*, VIII, 55-57.

citizens sought to outdo one another. To the private hatreds and enmities of families were added the disputes among the magnates, intent on restraining the advancement of the people, and the people, struggling to escape, by violence if necessary, from the criminal acts and usurpations of the magnates. To Dante this life of material interests and oppression was distasteful; there are echoes of his grief in the canzoni dealing with nobility and true love courtship, and also in a sonnet addressed to Cino da Pistoia.* But, as we expect of great minds, he did not withdraw from the conflict. The new ordinances of Florence (1293) had left a scant share of the government indeed to the nobles who did not actually exercise a craft (*arte*), even though there were no *grandi* who were under compulsion to provide special guarantees to the republic. But on July 6, 1295, a partly attenuating constitutional provision granted nobles of a certain rank the privilege of being elected to the councils of the people and to the priorate, conditional only upon simple registration on the rolls of the guilds. Dante put forward his name, surely as a devotee of philosophic pursuits, to the guild of physicians and apothecaries. He was thus enabled to serve on the special council of the people for the half-year running from the first of November, 1295, to the thirtieth of April, 1296. He was summoned on December 14, 1295, from among the wise men of the various quarters of the city to take part at a council for the election of priors. He belonged also to the Council of the Hundred, which passed upon finances and affairs of the more important sort, from May till September in 1296, and to yet another council (we do not know which) in 1297.[7]

We do not have the minutes of the proceedings of the councils from July, 1298, to February, 1301; there is, however, avail-

---

* *Minor Poems,* LXXXII, "Le dolci rime d'amor ch'io solia"; LXXXIII, "Poscia ch'Amor del tutto m'ha lasciato"; XCVI, "Perch'io non trovo chi meco ragioni."

able other evidence of Dante's participation in the municipal government. In May, 1300, he was sent as an ambassador to San Gimignano for the purpose of inviting that commune to send her magistrates to an assembly of the Guelph communes of Tuscany in order to renew their alliance and select their commander in chief. It does not seem to have been in itself an office of much importance, but it must have meant much to Florence to maintain a close alliance with the Guelph communes of the region so that together they might defend a common independence, not against the usual demands of the Empire (which at that time was regarded as vacant, since Albert of Austria had not yet been recognized and crowned) but in opposition to Pope Boniface VIII, who, profiting from the vacancy and from the strifes of the Florentines, aspired to subject the whole of Tuscany to the rule of the Church. The trust placed in Dante in the face of that peril is confirmed by the fact that when the office of prior was open, he was elected to it for the two-month period from June 15 to August 15. The previous priorate had been the first to call attention to the pontiff's aims and had also been the first to attack them, without allowing itself to be frightened by threats of excommunication. And, since the method of election to the priorate was varied with each successive election, it is certain that everything was so arranged as to bring into office those persons who, it was thought, were required by the crisis. Thus, for the entire two months, Dante found himself opposing the schemes of the Roman Curia which, invoking the doctrine of *plenitudo potestatis* and grounding itself on the claims of the pope to act as vicar during vacancies of the imperial office, wished to interfere in matters of municipal jurisdiction. He found himself trying to counteract the secret schemes of Cardinal d'Acquasparta, dispatched as papal legate to Florence. The Signory took so firm a stand that on July 22 the pope, provoked by its resistance, instructed his legate to proceed against the Florentine governors, the priors, and the councils, excommunicating them, suspending them from office, confiscating their goods, annulling their credit, and the like. Dante was saved from excommunication only because the legate, deceived by some hope or other, forebore to hurl his spiritual thunderbolts until the end of September when a new group of priors had entered upon their duties.

A notable event at the beginning of Dante's tenure of office was the attack made by certain magnates, doubtless of the Black faction, during St. John's Eve upon the consuls of the guilds who were on their way to make the customary offering to the patron saint. The opposing faction was not slow in reacting against this attack. On the advice of Dante, it seems, the administration took this opportunity to enact a measure which aimed to free the city of the more riotous men, mainly the Blacks who seemed more inclined to gratify the wishes of Pope Boniface than to defeat their opponents. It condemned to banishment the ringleaders of both factions; among the exiles of the White faction was Dante's earliest friend, Guido Cavalcanti.[8] The rift in the city was thenceforward so deep that even "the clergy could not avoid siding heart and soul with one or the other of the two factions."[9] There were very few public-spirited citizens, men without partisan bias, who cared more for the welfare of their city than for the interests of their family or party. Of these, however, Dante was one. But in politics it seems necessary for people to "get together," you must always be "with" somebody, and it was out of the question to dream of a party of "neutrals," who, without maintaining any dubious relations themselves, would possess the power to compel the rest to stick by their duty. Dante joined that faction which seemed the more humane, the more capable of adjustment, the more tolerant,[10] even if the more

14 THE LIFE OF DANTE ALIGHIERI

feeble and the less alert, and took his stand with the Cerchi, the so-called "Whites." Pope Boniface also tried out the Cerchi, but in the face of the irresolution of Vieri, from then on felt obliged to think that it was inexpedient "to lose men for the sake of chits of women"; the men whom he was looking for he found in Corso Donati and in other blackguards of his own party.[11] Sure of their coöperation, he had already determined to induce the French prince, Charles of Valois, to recover Sicily and to subdue the rebels of Tuscany as well.[12] It was natural, then, that Dante, desirous of shaking off from his city the paramount dominion of the Church and the governance of Corso and his party, should confirm himself in his resolution of opposing the aims of Boniface VIII with all his strength.

Since, as we have already noted, there is an unfortunate gap in the council records, we cannot ascertain whether Dante held any other office between August, 1300, when his term expired, and February, 1301. Quite apart from his political activities we must reckon his election in April, 1301, by choice of the interested parties, as superintendent of the works necessary for the straightening and widening of the Strada di San Prócolo, purely for the convenience of the neighboring property owners and at their private expense. It is probable, however, that on March 15 of the same year, in a council in which he may have taken part as one of the "wise men" (*savi*) who had been summoned to it, he opposed the allocation of a subsidy to King Charles of Anjou for the reconquest of Sicily. A little later, on April 14, he was again called to determine the method of choosing priors. One of the proposals advanced by the papal legate was that they be chosen by lot from those nominated by the two parties; the welfare of the city demanded instead that men of doubtful honesty or those favoring the policy of the Roman Curia should not be nominated.

From April 1 to September 30 he was again a member of the Council of the Hundred; on June 19, the question twice arose whether it was necessary to continue giving to the pope the services of a hundred soldiers, an assistance which already had been granted for an expedition against the Aldobrandeschi on the borders of Tuscany; on each occasion Dante *consuluit quod de servitio faciendo domino Papae nichil fiat*. On September 13 he spoke up at a gathering of the united Councils *et aliorum bonorum virorum* on measures to be taken for the protection of the Ordinances of Justice and the Statutes of the People (that is, he spoke in one of those meetings which were usually held when serious events threatened the city, and it was necessary to grant full powers to the Signory); the notarial recorder of the proceedings has not preserved his opinion for us.

At the approach of Charles of Valois in October, 1301, the commune decided to send an embassy to Boniface to counteract the wicked schemes of the Blacks; Dante was one of the three chosen to go. Thus he had an opportunity to approach the great pontiff and to become acquainted with his court. He was there longer than he expected, for, shortly after the ambassadors arrived, Boniface sent the other two back to persuade the Florentines to humble themselves before him and to convince them that the peace of the city was the pope's only wish. With him he kept Dante, from whom he had most to fear."[13] Dante was thus prevented from participating in the irresolute, weak, and inconclusive policy followed by the Whites in the last months of their rule; such policy, coupled with the cowardice of the Cerchi when the time came for them to sharpen their weapons, led to the triumph of the opposition. Dante's house seems to have been one of the first to be plundered in the ascendancy of the Blacks during their initial revenge against their enemies. He probably never again returned to Florence. He was in Rome and later in Siena when word first reached him of the reversal suffered by his party. The first sentence overtook him in Siena on January 27, 1302. He and four others were condemned to pay 5,000 florins, to be banished for two years, and to be perpetually barred from public office under the all-inclusive charge of graft, embezzlement, opposition to the pope and Charles of Valois, disturbance of the peace of Florence, and turning over control of Pistoia to the Whites with the resultant expulsion of the Blacks, the faithful and devoted adherents of Holy Church. Since he failed to report in order to pay the fine and to defend himself within the assigned time, there followed a second sentence on March 10, applicable also to fourteen other citizens, which ordered that if he should ever come into the hands of the commune, he should be burned alive (*igne comburatur sic quod moriatur*).

There is no need to inquire of what in particular Dante could have been accused. Each of the accused men was forced to take the blame for the entire policy of the White faction, and each objection was met with the quibbling distinction *ipsi vel ipsorum aliquis*. Everyone understood that it was useless to plead his case in person and accepted the consequences of his failure to appear.

The Early Years of Exile

Exile widened Dante's horizon and made, out of a Florentine, a citizen of Italy. This is not to say that Florence in those days was a small observation post as compared with other Italian cities, nor that Dante failed to feel homesick for his beloved birthplace from which he had been cast out because of his love for her independence and peace, nor that he did not attempt, in those early days, along with his companions in misfortune, to retrieve what he had lost. We find him in 1302 at San Godenzo in the Mugello pledging security to the Ubaldini for the damages which they might receive in their war against Florence; in 1303 at Forlì as aide and secretary to Scarpetta Ordelaffi, and at Verona as ambassador to the Scaligers; writing and working as one of the twelve councillors of the White party in 1304 during the peace negotiations conducted by Cardinal da Prato between Florence and the exiles. But very soon he broke with the "wicked and stupid" company with whom he had fallen into banishment and took to forming a party by himself. From the testimony given by the author of the *Ottimo Commento* and from Dante's own words,* it seems that the breach was caused by serious charges and grudges of the party against him. We know nothing definitely, but Dante's nature was not such as to adjust itself easily to the opinion and the schemes of a crowd of factious partisans motivated by as many diverse interests as the group with which he found himself living and working.

He took refuge with the lords of Verona, but did not stay there long. A few years later he wrote that for him the world was his fatherland just as the sea is the common country of fishes;† and he lamented having had to go "through almost every part of the land where the Italian language extends, a pilgrim, almost a beggar," like a "vessel without sail or rudder, carried to various ports and river mouths and shores by the dry wind that wretched poverty breathes forth," and he mourned having been forced to show himself in such a pitiable state to many who perhaps had, owing to his reputation, imagined him to be in better circumstances; in their sight not

---
* *Par.*, XVII, 61–65; *Inf.*, XV, 70–72.
† *De Vulg. Eloq.*, I, vi, 3.

only did he now "suffer a lowering of personal prestige, but all his work as well became of less worth, both what he had already done and what he was yet to do."*

Now that he had parted company from his co-partisans, Dante's status was approximately that of a courtier only. His lot was to go from place to place, to the houses of the great lords who were famous for their generosity toward men of genius and learning or of pleasing personality. The liberality of the great nobles served as a means of bringing honor and useful retainers to their courts, or at least of securing entertainment in their daily lives. Dante's fate was thus to be compelled to live among a medley of people who came and went, and who were endowed with varying temperaments, tastes, and motives; all the way from persons of knowledge and political experience down to fools. The buffoons, indeed, were not the least welcome among the guests, nor the least profusely rewarded, nor the first to be asked to leave. That a man of Dante's disposition, penetrated with a sense of his own worth, should feel at ease in such an atmosphere is not even faintly to be imagined, even if we had not enough sad evidence against it in his works.† His invective in the *De Vulgari Eloquentia*‡ against the princes of his time is plain enough.

We understand how such a life might make him feel more keenly the yearning for his native city and all the cherished things that he had left behind. The thought that, because of a measure enacted in Florence in 1303, even his sons, upon reaching the age of fourteen, would be forced to share his fate, must have troubled him greatly. There was a time when he was reduced to "humility, seeking through good works and good behavior to be allowed to return to Florence through a

---

* *Conv.*, I, iii, 4–5.
† *Par.*, XVII, 58–60; *Conv.*, I, vi, 3.
‡ *De Vulg. Eloq.*, I, xii, 5.

voluntary recall by those who ruled the land; and with this idea in view he exerted himself, and wrote more than once not only to individual members of the government, but also to the people. Among these letters is a very extended one which begins "Popule mee, quid feci tibi?"¹⁴ And to Florence he sent a canzone in which he praises her love for justice, in order that she might work with the citizens to win him peace. One line of that poem proclaims that "forgiveness is the most beautiful victory."* If his people did not forgive him, it was because they did not know the kind of man he was; because they did not know that he endured unjust exile for no other reason than for having loved Florence.† It had been easy to brand him as an enemy of the city. His opposition to the policy of the Church; the judicial sentence which is always a presumption of guilt; the fact that the true Ghibellines who had already been banished from Florence had joined with the White exiles in the first attempts to reconquer their homeland; his having had to seek refuge and assistance in cities of Tuscany and Romagna inimical to the Guelph party—all this had soon caused public opinion to associate him and his friends with the Ghibellines. Now, by keeping at a distance from the enemies of Florence, by living in places which were not suspect, by defending in his epistles what he had done for his city and the Guelph party when he fought at Campaldino against the Ghibellines, and by protecting the independence of the commune against every foreign interference whether imperial or otherwise, Dante bent every effort toward freeing himself of the charge of Ghibellinism and of opposition to the traditional policy of Guelph Florence.

But no less useful for his recall, he thought, might be the

---
* *Minor Poems*, CIV, 101-107, "Tre donne intorno al cor mi son venute".
† *Ibid.*, CIV, 105; *De Vulg. Eloq.*, I, vi, 3.

composition of a substantial and learned work which would show the world that he was something more than a mere versifier. Such a work would also help him to find worthy employment which would free him from degrading poverty and from the necessity of wandering like a beggar from place to place. In the *Vita Nuova* he had already sought to distinguish himself and his friend from "certain uncouth" poets who wrote their verses at random rather than according to reason and art; but it was necessary to demonstrate better that if he had cultivated poetry in the vernacular, it had not been for want of skill and study. It had been his intention to apply to vernacular poetry the practices, the criteria of the "regular" poets, that is, of the Latin poets. In writing vernacular poems he had not only expressed his amatory responses to feminine beauty or the passions suitable to youth, but by availing himself of the poet's privilege to represent ideal and elevated objects under the guise of sensuous appearances he had celebrated, in the conventional love patterns, his ardor for study and his reverence for philosophy and for themes bearing on civic education. Indeed, in justice, he deserved to be called "the poet of righteousness." Hence, the two treatises (which were left incomplete), the *De Vulgari Eloquentia* and the *Convivio*. We may assign their composition to the years 1304-1307. These works clearly evince both his determination to reëstablish his reputation impaired by exile, by reacting with every possible means against the ill-fortune which harassed him, and his desire to find a solace for his sorrows in the study of, and in writing about, matters useful to man's welfare and to art.*

---

* *Conv.*, I, ii, 15-17; iv, 13; ix, 7; *De Vulg. Eloq.*, I, xvii, 6.

The Origin of the Great Poem

Dante's horizons did not brighten. In such persistent adversity, his mind was of necessity diverted from the ideals of courtesy and love cherished in his youth and from knowledge, eagerly pursued as the perfection of human nature and a guide to the ethical improvement of the individual, toward more tangible problems of politics.

The world was without justice, without peace; there were laws, but no one who had either the power of enforcing them or an interest in doing so; greed, envy, violence were everywhere triumphant. Wherever his harsh exile drove him throughout Italy, Dante found other unhappy persons who had been cast out of their cities; nowhere did he find orderly, peaceful government; quarrels, oppression, and the despotism of factions or usurpers raged on all sides; there were conflicts and wars between neighboring cities. Pondering the causes of so much evil, he thought he saw the principal reason for it in the lack of a supreme ruler to bring the multifarious wills into unity, who, possessing everything and having nothing to wish for, might check the covetousness of others. Divine providence (until then he had failed to notice this)* had ordained the Roman Empire for this office; but the emperors of Dante's epoch, detained by other demands upon them in Germany, had not carried out their chief duty, which was to come to Italy to cure the blight in the garden of the Empire and to rule the world from Rome. Moreover, they were hindered in their actions by the Church, which, instead of fulfilling the obligation divinely entrusted to her, of guiding Christians to eternal deliverance, meddled in temporal affairs. Aspiring to supremacy over the Empire, the Church claimed paramount

---
* Cf. *Mon.*, II, i, 2–3.

power as her due in both the spiritual and the temporal realm. Such a situation resulted in the disastrous conflict between the two divinely ordained guides, the Empire and the Papacy. A breed of unscrupulous criminals profited by that conflict; and greed spread through the bad example set by the Roman See which seemed to be more concerned with temporal power and earthly goods than with its apostolic role and the salvation of souls.

Dante's desire and resolve to begin a work different from the one he was then engaged in must have developed simultaneously with this change in his thought. It was to be a work which would portray the ravages of such widespread depravity and which would persuade people to mend their ways and to return to the right path. The *Convivio* and the *De Vulgari Eloquentia* were in consequence interrupted. A plan was again taken up which Dante, for an entirely different reason, had cherished as early as the days when his mind had had time to dwell upon the contemplation of the blessed Beatrice in the court of heaven.* Nothing would be easier, now, than to insert new ideas into the old scheme, to combine the glorification of the beloved woman, who was watching from heaven over his earthly trials, with the poetical portraiture of a world misguided for so many reasons and in so many ways gone astray. The effects of so great a perversion and the deserving virtue of one person who could keep himself immune from the world's taint might better be shown in the other existence than in this one. From the other world the reader would receive warnings about this world, instruction, and best of all, examples.† The effectiveness of these would be all the greater, the more adequately they expressed the belated repentance of the sinner or the assurance of one who henceforth sees all in

---
* Cf., *Vita Nuova*, XLII, 1-2.
† *Par.*, XVII, 136-142.

God. A treatise like the *Convivio* was not enough to divert Italy from evil; nor could epistolary exhortations to kings or emperors, to princes or cities, do it. What right had he, a private citizen, exiled from his homeland, persecuted by adverse destiny, to hope that he would be heard? He could derive authority to speak only from his genius as a poet. A great vision was needed in which the immensity of evil could be portrayed in colors sufficiently vivid to make an impression in both high and low places; a vision in which the meaning, the instruction, would arise from the history of humanity in its eventful development and not from contingent or unimportant matters; a vision in which the divine intention to intervene in the restoration of eternal law and the reëstablishment of the world upon its true course could be announced in solemn fashion. The work for which Dante is famous and to which he dedicated all the remaining years of his life was thus conceived. In accordance with the learning of his time he called it merely the *Comedy* because of the plain style in which he starts out and because of its subject, sorrowful at the beginning and joyful at the end. It remained for posterity to call it a *Divine Comedy*.

The Descent of Henry VII

We do not know where Dante stayed longest after he left his companions in exile. We know only that in 1306 he was hospitably entertained by the Malaspina marquesses* in whose behalf he had carried on negotiations with the Bishop of Luni, and succeeded in settling their differences. There is no real evidence, and it seems improbable, that he crossed the Alps

---

* Cf. *Purg.*, VIII, 124–132.

to go to Paris, lured by that famous center of philosophical and theological studies.

After the descent into Italy of Henry VII had been announced and had taken place in 1310, for three years Dante lived in anxious expectation of the emperor's great undertaking. The latter's arrival was heralded as that of a *rex pacificus* who came down into the peninsula to restore harmony between cities and factions, to reinstate the exiles in their homelands, to quell the usurpations of government, to reestablish agreement between the Church and the Empire. Actually, he enjoyed the reputation of a just and holy man, desirous of the public good; and the pope, since he had favored Henry's election, appeared to be perfectly in accord with him and urged the people of Italy to welcome him with open arms. All the exiles were immediately on his side. How could Dante keep from opening his mind to hope? How could he withhold his approval of one who did not wish to hear of Guelphs and Ghibellines, and who seemed concerned only with reconciling differences and with rendering justice to all? What more had he been asking for so many years? His first outburst came in a noble letter to the kings, princes, and people of Italy: "Rejoice, sorrowful Italy, for thy bridegroom hastens to the marriage, and you that weep oppressed, lift up your hearts, because your salvation is nigh; and all of you, Italians, rise to meet your king, as people reserved not only for his empire, but for his direct governance."*

As we have already noted, in his studies Dante had gradually become convinced of the need for universal empire as the only agency which could transcend individual interests, weigh with justice the inevitable dissensions between city and city, kingdom and kingdom, and secure by timely legislation

---

* *Epist.*, V, 2, 5, 6, *passim*.

and just decisions the peace essential to the well-being of the world.

No sooner did Henry cross the boundaries of Italy than Dante hurried to pay homage: "I have seen thee most gracious and have heard thee most clement, when my hands touched thy feet and my lips paid their debt."* Although Dante foresaw the reluctance of Florence to recognize the authority of the emperor, fearful prudence did not keep him from setting out resolutely upon his path. Truth and the public good above all! What would it matter if the Empire were in the hands of a German king? He had been chosen by providence; with the coronation in Rome he would become a citizen of Italy, and from Rome he would govern the peninsula and rule the world. The duties of the imperial office, which other kings of the Romans had neglected, Henry wanted to perform without hesitation and with the best intentions. What citizen, heedful of his duties, could deny him approval? or worse, oppose him? And since Florence, fearing in the emperor a barbarian king who might be hostile to the liberties laboriously won by the communes, a tyrant levying taxes and duties, not only resisted Henry, but also, full of arrogance and freehanded with florins, aroused almost all Italy against the invader, a new conflict between Dante and his city was inevitable. He hurled the thunderbolts of his anger against the wicked Florentines within the city in a letter addressed to them. While Henry lingered in northern Italy overcoming other opposition, here was Dante, fearless and as though moved by prophetic ardor, to warn him that the real danger was not there, and to spur him into rushing to wipe out the hydra of the rebellion on the Arno. Florence retaliated by including Dante's name among the exceptions to the amnesty granted by a pro-

---
* *Ibid.*, VII, 9.

vision of September, 1311, known as the Reform of Baldo d'Aguglione."

However, when Henry finally decided to follow Dante's advice, the latter refused to fight against his native city, so much did his love for Florence restrain him from bearing arms in an undertaking which was to be, if not destruction, an exemplary punishment of the rebellious city. His name, in fact, does not appear among those of the Florentines sentenced for having been on the side of the emperor. He seems not to have discharged any official duties for Henry; his letters written at this time are dated from the Casentino where he apparently enjoyed the hospitality of the Count of Battifolle. Dante's contribution to the emperor's expedition was his nobly courageous support, and of course, his impetuous exhortations. Later, when to the opposition of Florence was added that of King Robert," and finally, both secretly and openly, that of Pope Clement V, it is probable that in defense of the unacknowledged and opposed imperial rule he set himself to writing the *De Monarchia* wherein he undertook to prove that the Empire was necessary to the welfare of the world, that it was God's gift to the people of Rome, and that imperial power was independent of the supreme religious authority.

The Last Years

Even before Henry's death, Dante had begun to doubt that the redemption of Italy was destined to be Henry's task; but for all that the unexpected death of the emperor was a serious blow. The poet faced his new misfortune with resolute mind, firmer than ever in his conviction about the role of the Empire and that of the Church, and about the reasons for the evils that plagued Italy and the world. His letter to the Italian cardinals after the death of Clement V in 1314 is an impassioned plea to succor Rome, which had formerly been happy and renowned because of the two suns that cast their light upon her, a light the splendor of which was reflected upon all Christian lands. Now the imperial city was deprived of both her suns. The Italian cardinals, especially the Roman ones, should, by electing a pope from their own country, put an end to the disgrace of the papacy at Avignon and should restore to Italy and Rome the glory usurped by others.

There was a time when his relatives and friends hoped that Dante might be able to return to his city by accepting one of those amnesties to which the city of Florence resorted either to lessen the number of her foreign enemies or for purely financial reasons. In 1315 a certain person urged him to take advantage of a repeal of his sentence, one of the conditions of this sentence being that he should present himself as an oblate to St. John on the saint's feast day that year. This form of penance applicable to noble persons, was practiced in cases of acknowledged error, and the most humiliating formalities, such as wearing a bishop's miter while walking in procession to the church of the patron saint, were excluded." But Dante, the disdainful exile and the friend of justice, refused to return to Florence by any such means.

In August of that year, after the rout of Montecatini, the Florentine commune was compelled to consider other ways of getting back the least dangerous of its exiles, not by acquitting them of their offenses but by commuting their death sentences to confinement to certain areas, provided the exiles would give their word to remain in the places designated. Dante was among these, and of course he would not accept. Not having answered the new judicial summons by October

15, on November 6 he was again condemned to death, this time with his sons who, as offspring of a rebel, were henceforth joined with their father in a common fate.

We do not know just where and how the poet spent the last eight years of his life. Did he remain in the Casentino or did he take refuge with Uguccione della Faggiuola immediately after Uguccione's successful undertakings gave Dante hope that he would be luckier than Henry was against Florence?[16] Or did he appeal to the generosity of Cangrande della Scala soon after the death of the emperor; and if the fortunes of Uguccione detained him for a while in Tuscany, was this a more or less brief interruption of the hospitality of the Scaligers? And was it from Tuscany, or from Verona that he went to Ravenna, that tranquil haven of his last years? The opinions and arguments of the critics are many, the evidence doubtful; it is not, however, a matter of great importance. What seems certain is that Dante sought and found a relative security and peace in the last years of his life. He was able to have his children with him, and whatever may be thought to the contrary, probably even his wife. There is also the question of whether he held a lectureship on poetry and rhetoric in Ravenna for a time; actually, if the constraining power of circumstances led him to accept such an office, such was his fame that in 1320 he did not need a doctor's degree in order to give a lecture at Verona before the assembled clergy, publicly settling the question, which had arisen while he was in Mantua, of the location and nature of the two elements, water and earth. At Verona and Ravenna he devoted himself particularly to finishing the poem with which he expected to bring about his honorable recall to Florence; it was barely completed when, returning from a mission to Venice on behalf of Guido da Polenta, Dante died on September 13 or 14, in the year 1321.

He was buried in Ravenna with great honor in a stone tomb

THE LIFE OF DANTE ALIGHIERI 29

in a chapel near the church first named after San Pier Maggiore and later called San Francesco; his bones, though often sought by the Florentines, still rest in that chapel, now converted into a small shrine by the veneration of posterity.

About his person, Boccaccio wrote: "Our poet was of medium height; he had a long face, an aquiline nose, large jaws, and his lower lip was more prominent than the upper; he was slightly stoop-shouldered, and his eyes were large rather than small; his coloring was dark; his hair and beard were curly and black, and he seemed always melancholy and thoughtful." But among the many portraits, miniatures, and sculptures that have come down to us, none is completely trustworthy. The most reliable ones present two types: one, a youthful face, is the fresco by Giotto in the palace of the podestà in Florence; the other, the likeness of a mature man, is supposedly a copy of a painting by Taddeo Gaddi in Santa Croce.[2] The portrait by Giotto has been entirely repainted, but fortunately two tracings of it were made in 1842 by Seymour Kirkup and Perseo Faltoni. The second type, the mature man, is the more common one which has become traditional through the centuries; even Raphael conforms to this type in that vigorous figure of the poet included in the *Dispute of the Sacrament*.

After the death of Dante, the sentence of banishment against his sons should have been annulled; however, they had been referred to as his sons, without actually being named, in the banishment of 1315, and this gave rise to uncertainties about their legal status in the commune of Florence. Gemma was able to reclaim her dowry rights to the confiscated estate of her husband; Beatrice became a nun at San Stefano degli Olivi in Ravenna. Iacopo soon returned to his homeland; assured of his status through an amnesty of 1325, he continued to live thereafter in Florence although he retained his benefices in Verona. With only modest talent he set himself to explaining and glossing the *Commedia* (which, with excusable pride, he calls his sister); the work is always superficial and indicates that he was far from understanding his father's mind and art; he was also occupied with writing a prosy *Dottrinale* of moral and scientific subject matter. Pietro appears in Florence in 1323 and 1324, and in Bologna in 1327 as a student of civil law, but settled later in Verona where he held the office of judge until he died in 1364 at Treviso. He left behind a family line which ended in the Serego Alighieri. Pietro also commented upon the *Divina Commedia* several times in Latin; he was perhaps endowed with more learning than Iacopo, but with no greater knowledge of his father's thought and purpose.

Part II
The Minor Works

The Minor Works and the "Trilogy"

Dante's fame rests on the *Divina Commedia*. But even his minor works, in addition to being indispensable for a better understanding of that poem, are in one way or another useful in the history of culture and art. Some scholars have come to believe that two of these minor works, the *Vita Nuova* and the *Convivio,* constitute, together with the great poem, a real trilogy. However, to admit this, all three works would have to be completed and articulated with one another like the three acts of a play. Instead, the *Convivio* was interrupted to make way for the *Divina Commedia:* moreover, in spite of all the efforts made by critics, no one has succeeded in reconciling the data of the three works. The connections between them are explained by two's: the *Convivio* was really conceived as a sequel and development of the *Vita Nuova;* and the *Commedia* (so far as Beatrice is concerned) presupposes a knowledge of what that gentle lady meant in the life of Dante, and hence the writing of the *Vita Nuova* itself; but a deliberate connection and coördination of the three works so as to form a trilogy does not exist.

There are other scholars who, having abandoned the idea of a literary trilogy, persist in discovering three periods in the inner life of Dante, of which the *Vita Nuova*, the *Convivio*, and the *Commedia* would be the artistic expressions, respectively, of an early period of guileless faith and deep mysticism; a second, of rationalism and unrestrained life; and a third period characterized by the return to a profoundly religious life and an enlightened faith. But whoever sees a state of burning mysticism in the youthful life of Dante is viewing it entirely from the viewpoint of the *Vita Nuova;* that is, from a moment of special and imaginative exaltation produced in the poet by repentance for an early infidelity toward the memory of his Beatrice. Traces of that exaltation in poems written before that time are but expressions of transitory moods which this or that poem has recorded. But actually both the life and the youthful poetry of Dante are more varied than critics are disposed to believe. As for the *Convivio,* it is vain to seek in it evidences of rationalism: there are, on the contrary, continuous proofs of the subjection of reason to revealed truth, and of Dante's longing for an enlightened faith triumphant over every doubt. In this respect the work in prose does not differ from the *Divina Commedia.*

Two events have made an impression on the critics; the death of Beatrice and the death of Henry VII. They certainly are important moments in Dante's life. Neither one in itself was, however, sufficient to determine a crucial change in his thought and convictions. Before God decided to call her to Himself, Beatrice was already a creature of heaven and a guide to eternal salvation; and the mission on which Dante had embarked as a citizen and poet underwent no change because of the hope, now lost, which he had placed in the supreme ruler. Nor is it to be expected, in such a complex and troubled life as that of Dante's, that everything should have developed regularly and continuously without contradictions and backslidings. We should be strictly on our guard against mistaking certain confusions of restless, troubled minds as permanent mental conditions, and against misapprehending momentary desires for persistent feelings and aims. Above all, we must not yield to the tendency of our own minds toward constructions along clear-cut, precise lines. If we must admit that there are three periods in Dante's life, they may be distinguished thus: first, by the cultivation of amatory poetry and the chivalric ideal; second, by his enthusiasm for knowledge as the real perfection of man; and third, by the desire for a politico-religious reform and by the self-assumed mission as prophet and seer at the time of his life when, witnessing the misdirected politics of his age, brought about principally by the malfeasance of the popes, he had realized that humanity had strayed from both the right road of the earthly life and the right road of the heavenly hereafter. To the first period would belong the *Vita Nuova,* those of the early poems that were not included in it, and many of the poetical compositions that he continued to write after its completion; to the second, the allegorical and doctrinal poems, the *De Vulgari Eloquentia* and the *Convivio;* to the third, the epistles written on the occasions of Henry's arrival in Italy and the conclave of 1314, the *De Monarchia* and the *Commedia.*

The Vita Nuova

The *Vita Nuova* is a collection of poems linked by prose passages (*ragioni*) that explain the occasion of each poem, and supplied with glosses that clarify their meaning. No other work has given rise to such a variety of opinions. Is it a more or less faithful, more or less idealized story of Dante's youthful love affairs, and in particular the story of that love for Beatrice which absorbed all others? Or are Beatrice and the gentle Lady, who for a while takes her place, pure allegorical depictions of sentimental and ideal aspirations, and similar to his inclination toward a simple faith and the worship of philosophy which contend for dominance in the soul of the poet? And granting that the praise of Beatrice does not exceed the bounds of amatory poetry, does this work deal with the love of a real woman to whom Dante paid customary homage, or does it deal with the glorification of an ideal lady whom the poet portrays after a conceptual pattern rather than from the faces of women who appear to him at various times in his life? And again, is it a work that was conceived and composed *per se,* independently of the others, or was it planned at an early date and later adjusted to other works like the *Convivio* and the *Commedia?* And if so, when was the work first written down, when were the alterations made?

The most trustworthy opinion among so many guesses is that the *Vita Nuova* is to be read literally without hidden meanings, and that it has never had any other form than the one we know; and since the facts related in it do not take us beyond 1292, the plan and the completion of it must not have occurred much later than that year. If we fail to take into account the poet's psychological mood on the return of his affections and thoughts to Beatrice after his brief infatuation with the compassionate Lady, we cannot understand the work, nor perceive its spiritual and aesthetic unity. This unity results entirely from the vivid coloring and from the special significance which the soul of the poet, looking back, in a moment of profound emotion, upon his past and viewing his life in a new light, bestows on the facts and on the poems composed at different times, with varying inspiration.

There is no doubt that because of this state of mind and because of his fervent eulogy of Beatrice as a creature sent to earth by God for the salvation of men (and particularly for

his guidance), Dante's early life seems suffused in the *Vita Nuova* with an aura of mysticism. Actually, the poet lived the life of his period and valued courtesy and valor as the necessary endowments of a gentleman; and to write of such things in poetry was to show that he was a follower of the "true courtship of love." More than any other work, the composition of the *Vita Nuova* is due to Dante's ardent wish to emerge as an artist fully conscious of his technical powers. The subject matter is common to vernacular poetry both in the language of *oc* and in the language of *sì*,[1] and it consequently remains within the precincts of the conventions of love poetry about real women: there is no hint of novelty in this respect where he speaks of the origin of "discoursing in rhyme."*
Even when, having detailed the occasion for each poem and having given the poem, he sets about commenting upon it in the manner of a schoolman, the only purpose of the gloss is to show that he is not one of those "coarse" versifiers who botch up poems in a slovenly fashion, but that instead he knows how to give a good account of his poetic images. Nor does the idealization of the woman differ at all from that praise of feminine virtues and beauty common to all love poetry. Where this idealization may seem to partake of transcendency, its function is, instead, to bring back to earth the ideal of human perfection; for nature creates human souls so perfect that they differ little from angels, and God gives to creatures such a measure of His grace as corresponds to the degree of worth with which nature has endowed them; so that it is not strange that even on earth there are souls that are almost divine.†

Some of the poems in the *Vita Nuova* are just the exercises of a beginning poet or an expression of conventional senti-

---

* *Vita Nuova*, XXV.
† *Conv.*, III, vii, 2–7; IV, xxi, 6–12.

ment; not a few of them, however, deserve the title "new rhymes" which their author gave to them because of their sincerity of inspiration and their originality of expression. And even where he takes over a conventional form of presentation, for example, the vision, Dante succeeds in creating a thing of new beauty, as in the canzone he wrote when he feared the approaching death of Beatrice, "Donna pietosa e di novella etate." He seems less bound to tradition in the prose parts which give their tone to all the rest and which justify the appropriateness of the designation *Vita Nuova*. There he shows that he was really inspired; and from that inspiration the work derives a freshness and originality of presentation which are noteworthy for that age. It is sufficient to recall such vivid episodes as the scene of the mockery, that of the gentlewomen eager to know the mystery of a love that is so different from Dante's other affairs, the procession of the pilgrims who are plunged in self-concern and regretful of their abandoned goods, but indifferent to the grief of the city through which they are passing. More amazing because of its poetic novelty is the episode of the piteous Lady: a temptation of love rather than a real love; a longing for new love, of some days' duration, which the poet mourns as though it were a serious infidelity, a despicable and wicked thing; an amorous inclination that is born of a gentlewoman's pity for his bereavement and that is depicted as the just comfort for his soul weary from long weeping, but is, instead, fought against and conquered by the holiness of his memories, and ends in remorse and a new affliction.

The *Vita Nuova* also has historical importance as a work which best establishes the characteristics of the school of the "new style" both in the concept of love and the concept of art (Dante speaks not only for himself, but also for Guido Cavalcanti, to whom the book is dedicated). It is, moreover, important for its literary form itself; a book of memories and confessions, which takes its place alongside the romances of courtly love and the knightly songs from beyond the Alps.

The Minor Poems

Not all of Dante's youthful poems were collected by him in the *Vita Nuova*. He excluded many that had been inspired by Beatrice and several that had been written for other women. He planned to assemble in the *Convivio,* fourteen canzoni, but we find only three of them in that work: the others that had already been marked for comment (there is a likelihood that he did not succeed in composing all the poems he had planned) were left out. These extraordinary lyrics, with others composed at various times in his life either as outlets for his emotions, as exercises in art, as part of his correspondence with other poets, or simply as a means of delighting ladies and gentlemen who were fond of poetry, make up what we call the *Canzoniere*. He made no attempt to organize them into a separate work, either because he had no time to do so or because the idea never occurred to him. Having turned to a great task in his artistic maturity, he attached less importance to the scattered poems of his youth and was probably dissuaded from such a plan by the partial collections he had already made in the *Vita Nuova* and the *Convivio:* they remained scattered in manuscript collections of old vernacular poetry, and became confused with the productions of other poets. Today it is difficult to sift the genuine from the aprocryphal and to arrange them according to epochs and inspiration. Some have been lost: for example, a *serventese* in praise of sixty Florentine ladies,* and a canzone which began "Tràggemi de la mente Amor la stiva."† His total poems scarcely number a hundred.

The "unattached" poems of Dante's youth have a double importance. They aid in the reconstruction of his inner life by furnishing details that either complement or correct those of the *Vita Nuova,* and they provide us with various manifestations of his art. There are gay and fanciful tones, as in the sonnets "Guido i' vorrei che tu e Lapo ed io" and "Sonar bracchetti e cacciatori aizzare." There are poems that have a playful, light, and musical character, as "Non mi poriano già mai fare ammenda" and "Per una ghirlandetta." There are canzoni of a passionate tone, very unlike that of the *Vita Nuova,* as "E' m'increase di me sì duramente" and "Lo doloroso amor che me conduce."

Among the occasional poems, those he exchanged with his fellow poets, particularly with Cavalcanti, are of great value, in that they show the part poetry played in Florentine life of the thirteenth century. They exemplify the ideals of life and art that inspired the group of poets who called themselves writers of the "new style." Noteworthy, too, is the debate with Forese Donati, started probably as a joke in a moment of idleness and good humor, and quickly transformed into a tit-for-tat of reproaches and coarse insults. There is no reason to infer from them a period of Dante's life characterized by libertinism. We may assume rather that in the narrow life of a city of that time his mind was not always employed upon a worthy and absorbing occupation, and that the manners of the age allowed of rather wide limits for jokes and insults.

Certain amatory poems of his maturity‡ dissuade us from

---

* *Vita Nuova,* VI, 2.
† *De Vulg. Eloq.* II, xi, 5.
‡ E.g., "Amor da che convien," and cf. *Epist.* IV.

viewing the following poems as allegorical, as many critics do: "Amor che movi," "Io sento sì d'Amor," "Io mi son pargoletta," "Chi guarderà già mai," and others;* for even when Dante devoted himself to study and politics, he continued to think it an ornamental accomplishment to write of love. Love to him was a virtue drawing all man's powers toward good actions; it was indeed the source of every virtue and every noble deed.† We are not saying that he did not attempt allegorical poetry in his maturity. On the contrary, he undertook to compose, in praise of philosophy, a type of poetry comprising not only canzoni but also sonnets and ballads, with a view to depicting philosophy's various seeming transformations during his efforts to conquer her. First he imagines philosophy as a gentle consoler of his grief over the loss of Beatrice, like the piteous Lady of the *Vita Nuova;* then he portrays philosophy as a hard and disdainful woman, obviously in reference to the difficulty that speculative studies present to him as his desire increases. Nor did he stop there; in spite of his original idea, voiced in the *Vita Nuova*,‡ that vernacular poetry should be limited to amatory poems, he added, in order to widen the range of his art, a certain number of canzoni in praise of the moral virtues, the visible beauties of philosophy.

A group of poems called the "stony" poems (because they exalt a woman—Pietra—hard as stone) assume a particular importance because of the problems they have constantly posed. Some scholars assign them to the year 1296; some to the years 1306 and 1307, and still others, to the year 1310; some argue that they reveal a real and turbulent passion by which the poet was overcome; to others, they are pure allegory, or

---

* Cf. Sonnets LXXXVI and XCVI, "Due donne in cima de la mente mia"; "Perch'io non trovo chi-meco ragioni."
† *Minor Poems*, XC, "Amor, che movi tua vertù dal cielo."
‡ *Vita Nuova*, XXV, 6.

simply experiments in art. And, indeed, the study of the poems of Arnaut Daniel which they reveal—the author's boasts that he has dared to produce novelties never before thought of—the content and form of the so-called canzoni,— everything taken together—leads us to assume that they are experiments. It was a prejudice of the times that art is an external thing, to be superimposed like an ornament upon the idea; and Dante shared it. To the true poet, ideas gleaned in any way, whether from his own experiences or from the expressions of others, are sufficient to give food to the creative imagination. As for the chronology, it is preferable to assign Dante's "stony" poems to the period before his exile.

Aside from the occasional poems, the *Canzoniere* constitutes a series of experiments made by a man who seeks progressively to satisfy the ceaseless and inmost needs of art and learning, as well as the requirements of moral instruction and those of education in "civics." Without departing from the usual form, Dante moves away from the tradition of writing on amatory matters and infuses his lyrics with a fresher inspiration and a bolder, more conscious art. In honor of his lady he collects, articulates, and comments upon the poems of his youth. After the loss of Beatrice, she is replaced by love, the source of every noble inspiration, every right action, and of knowledge itself; it is love that leads him to reverence every beautiful thing with the delight its beauty inspires, whether the object of his love be a real creature of virtue and charm, or a study of what perfects the mind and ennobles the spirit; whether the object of his love be a virtue or a specific doctrine. According to the ideas most commonly held at that time, poetry was viewed, above all, as *fictio rhetorica,* formal excellence, artistic perfection. This was achieved, particularly in the canzone, by the scrupulous selection of vocabulary and wisely contrived constructions; and the inspiration of love was not merely an emotion: it was a source of instruction; it was a phase of learning.

It may be said that Dante was determined to succeed where Guittone had failed, in harsh rhyming, in *trobar escur,* in purely doctrinal poetry. He clearly meant to show that he would dare anything in order to achieve the "glory of the language," writing poetry with that regular art which the Latin poets and the best troubadours of Provence exemplified. He did not succeed equally well in all his experiments, for not even his elevated imagination could suffice to transform pure doctrine into poetry; but none of his contemporaries could compete with him in novelty, variety, and boldness. Just as the sweet fancies of his youth gave us perfect sonnets like "Tanto gentile," and lyric inspiration wisely joined with dramatic portraiture resulted in a canzone like "Donna pietosa," so, in the poet's maturity, we also find canzoni worthy of him; it is sufficient to call to mind "Così nel mio parlar," where the passion of love is voiced in new and vigorous accents, and "Tre donne intorno al cor," where the noblest sentiments that move the human mind are expressed with unusual sublimity.

The Convivio

The *Convivio* was planned as a commentary on fourteen canzoni dealing both with love and the practical virtues. It was to consist of fifteen treatises, the first being an introduction to the work, and each of the others an explanation of one canzone. Only four were written, although provision for the others was made: in IV, xxvi, 8, he tells us what he will say in the seventh treatise; in I, xii, 12; II, i, 4 and IV, xxvii, 11, he tells us that in the fourteenth he will discuss allegory and justice; in I, viii, 18 and III, xv, 14 he alludes to the subjects on which he will discourse in the fifteenth. It has been conjectured that, after the fourth treatise, he meant to discuss the eleven moral virtues stemming from nobility;* but such a notion is extremely doubtful, since he may have found it expedient to comment upon other amatory canzoni that were already written. The fact remains that where he enumerates and defines the eleven virtues, he does not even hint at a more ample treatment to follow.

The work seems to be a continuation and development of the *Vita Nuova*. He takes up the story from the account of the compassionate Lady, without dwelling upon the fact that this affair had been a brief delight of the senses soon overcome by the memory of Beatrice. Here he intends to celebrate that greater and more enduring consolation which, through all the hardships of study, he had found in the love of philosophy, already portrayed in his canzoni as a woman of great beauty and virtue. In order to remove every disagreement between the two works, he took advantage of the medieval custom of explaining literary works according to four senses and attaching to the account an allegorical meaning which it originally did not possess. And in this way he thought he would accomplish two purposes: first, he would show that although he had spent a good part of his life writing of love, it was not because he was a man inclined to that passion by nature (even where he seemed to speak only of love, he was dealing with virtue and wisdom); second, by explaining the real meaning of his canzoni in the vernacular, that is, by expounding the doctrine hidden under the appearance of the letter, he would prepare a banquet of learning for those who, busied with civil matters and the governance of the commonwealth, either

---

* *Conv.*, IV, xvii, 4–7.

could not, or were not prepared to attend the schools. He would thus succeed in leading to knowledge and virtue "princes, barons, knights, and many other noble folk, not only men, but women,"* conversant with the "vulgar tongue, but not with Latin," so that both in civil affairs and in social life they might have that knowledge which would qualify them to be, as they ought to be, exemplary patterns of right behavior to the world.

He is, of course, a follower of Aristotelian philosophy, and he never tires of calling Aristotle the "teacher and leader of human reason,"† the philosopher "most worthy of faith and obedience,"‡ and of asserting that "where the divine opinion of Aristotle opens its mouth, the opinion of all other men should be disregarded."§ The commentaries of St. Thomas on the works of the Greek philosopher and the *Summa contra Gentiles* may be said to be his principal sources; he is no less familiar with Scriptures and the Latin writers including Seneca, Orosius, and Boethius; he is familiar with the most widely known Arabian commentaries on the works of Aristotle, perhaps through the references of other writers, rather than directly; he cites the *Confessions* of St. Augustine, the *De Meteoris,* the *De Coelo et Mundo,* and other works of Albertus Magnus; nor is it strange that he should know and quote the treatise *De Regimine Principum* of Egidio Colonna.

The fundamental truths of reason have all been made known to us by philosophers,** but the possibility of demonstrating new truths in both the speculative and the practical sphere is not to be excluded. As a result, scientific zeal is not wanting in the *Convivio;* there appears, rather, in every part

---
* *Ibid.,* I, ix, 5.
† *Ibid.,* IV, vi, 8.
‡ *Ibid.,* IV, vi, 6.
§ *Ibid.,* IV, xvii, 3.
** Cf. *Mon.* III, xvi, 9.

of it, the enthusiasm of a man who comes upon a new world and wishes, in his excitement, to have all others share his fortune. He wants to apply his new experiences to the requirements of contemporary life and to offer remedies where they are needed. His ideal of human life is so exalted that he realizes that very few persons in the world measure up to it; indeed, it seems at times as though everything has gone awry. But his faith remains unshaken. He is determined to recall those who have gone astray, and he feels great contempt for the rulers of nations who do not care to acquire that wisdom which is demanded by their office, or at least to surround themselves with men who might give them good advice.*

The importance of the *Convivio* lies not so much in the demonstration of Dante's philosophic learning as in the revelation of his personality. How he exalts learning! When he sets his mind to scanning the problem of the universe, how strongly he feels that reason is the truly ennobling attribute of man which draws him close to God! Dante does not himself sit at the blessed table of the sages, but, a fugitive from the pastures of the common herd, after tasting the sweetness of knowledge he wants his good fortune to be shared by those who have been hindered by domestic and civic pursuits from approaching scholarship and familiarizing themselves with it. And in order to be useful to the greatest possible number, with "ready liberality" he will employ, not the language of the schools, but the vernacular, the common speech, so greatly despised by those who do not know how to make good use of it. He stigmatizes those who find fault with the vernacular because they are basely envious of anyone who acquires renown by writing in it, as well as those who think they will earn more praise by using a foreign language, or who value, in their low minds, the possessions of others more than their

---

* *Conv.*, IV, vi, 19-20.

own. "Such are all those abominable wretches of Italy who debase this precious vernacular language that is of scant value only when it falls from the meretricious lips of these adulterers." Their example is followed by many others, the intellectually blind who, leaning with their hands upon the shoulders of these liars, fall "into the ditch of false opinion from which they cannot escape."* Dante, on the contrary, thundering out against "the perpetual shame and abasement" of those "wicked men of Italy who praise the vernacular of others and disparage their own," prefers it above all other tongues including Latin itself owing to his perfect love for Italian and his conviction of its intrinsic excellence. He hails its triumph with certainty: "This shall be the new light, the new sun which shall rise when the old one has set, and shall illuminate those who are in shadow and darkness because the wonted sun does not shed its beams on them."†

This new use of language was extraordinarily bold for those days, particularly because Dante dared to use his native speech in a learned and scholastic work like a commentary, for which Latin was by practically general consent prescribed. But his employment of the vernacular was essential to his plan of spreading knowledge through the pure and disinterested love that he professed for his mother tongue, a love so ardent as to lead him to deny the name of scholar to those who learn Latin in order to derive money and honor from it, whereas they should use it to acquire and to teach wisdom. For Dante this was tantamount to the prostitution of literature.‡ Philosophy must not result merely in wisdom; it must ennoble man's emotions and raise him to a higher way of life. From this conviction stems that elevated and

---

* *Ibid.*, I, xi, 1–21.
† *Ibid.*, I, xiii, 12.
‡ *Ibid.*, I, ix, 3–5.

(because of the evils Dante saw around him) severely passionate tone which pervades the *Convivio*.

Two tenets have a more personal "ring": the doctrine of nobility and that of the Empire. In the first we have a vindication of true nobility as a personal bent toward virtue, thanks to the operation of nature and of divine grace. Dante's theory is directed against those who would trace nobility to heredity or, worse, to a longstanding possession of wealth. It is repugnant to Dante, who has so high an ideal of human life, that such a privilege as nobility should consist merely of the obliteration, produced by time, of the obscurity and the base practices of ancestors. Nor should nobility be confused with so despicable a thing as wealth, which may be called good only so far as we deny it to ourselves in order to practice liberality. He boldly proclaims that "it is not the stock that ennobles the individuals, but the individuals the stock."* As for the Empire, he speaks of it only in passing,† but by way of showing the profound importance that is to be attached to such an office in the divine framework of the world. In the past, he had entertained a belief that the Roman Empire acquired universal rule not by right but by force;‡ now, turning a more penetrating glance on the succession of events, and examining the nature of things, he discerned in the advent of Empire a preordained plan of divine providence for the redemption of mankind and for its welfare in this earthly life. Thus the whole history of man became clear to him. The pages concerned with this subject vibrate with the enthusiasm of a first discovery. The formation of the Roman Empire as a preparation for the establishment of the Christian Faith he now solemnly affirmed without ever suspecting that another

---
* *Ibid.*, IV, xx, 5.
† *Ibid.*, IV, ii–v.
‡ *Mon.*, II, i, 2–3.

writer might use the same materials to arrive at conclusions denying the independence of the imperial office.

It is not to be assumed that the idea of the Empire possessed Dante's mind so profoundly when he began writing the *Convivio* as it did later. Although he saw the damage which was done to the peace and happiness of the world for want of a supreme ruler, this want, along with the usurpation of civil power by the Church, cannot have seemed to him to be the chief and most exclusive cause of every evil until at a somewhat later time in his life, when he thought all proposed remedies useless unless they provided for the reëstablishment of the order willed by God in the government of the world. It is true that among the causes that estrange most people from learning and hence from happiness,* he does not list the wars and conflicts which, for lack of good political rule, made his age most wretched. But he strongly emphasizes the importance of the "divine election of the Roman Empire,"† that by so potent an argument he may silence the disparagers of the supreme civil authority. And thus Rome becomes for him a holy thing for two reasons: (1) it is the seat of the Church of Christ, and (2) it is the home of the chosen people to whom, owing to their civic virtues, providence assigned the government of the world. "And doubtless," he concludes, "it is my firm opinion that the very stones of Rome's walls are worthy of reverence; and that the ground on which she stands is still more worthy than has been preached and proved by men."‡

---
* *Conv.*, I, i, 1–6.
† *Ibid.*, IV, v. 6.
‡ *Ibid.*, IV, v, 20.

De Vulgari Eloquentia

The same feeling which moved Dante to exalt the Italian vernacular in the *Convivio* prompted him also to try to give it a firm footing and to bestow upon it the same regularity as Latin, in the *De Vulgari Eloquentia*. He meant to go on writing this last work simultaneously with the *Convivio,* but he did not have as many reasons for writing it in the vernacular as he had stated existed for his commentary on the canzoni. The new treatise was addressed, not to princes and gentlemen, but to people of scholarly tastes, and could and should, therefore, be written in the language of the schools. The first book and a considerable part of the second were written; he refers to a fourth book in II, iv, 1; we do not know whether that book was to be the last.

In the first book he deals with language in general, first with its origin and then with its history, with sound judgment and an insight (though not without certain medieval prejudices) which assign him a high place among the precursors of modern linguistic science; and as he passes from national languages and, particularly, from those spoken in Spain, France, and Italy, to the dialects peculiar to the various regions of Italy, the novelty and value of his treatment increase. He even attempts a classification of the Italian dialects, with a view not only of establishing distinctions among them, but also of grouping them, a plan without precedent even in other countries. The appraisal of the various dialects is made with reference to that language which the writer was seeking to fix, that is, with reference to the "illustrious language" common to all Italy which was to be used for the noblest prose, and in poetry, for the canzone. When he compared these dialects to his literary ideal, he found something to be condemned, more or less, in all the vernacular tongues of Italy, in the Tuscan and Florentine dialect as well as the others. The "illustrious" vulgar tongue, or as he also calls it, the "cardinal, courtly, and curial vulgar tongue," is to be discerned faintly in this or that region or city, but resides in its entirety in none. He had in mind the language in which were couched, in transcriptions by Tuscan copyists, the poems of the most renowned writers of the Sicilian school. It was also the language of Guido Guinizelli, evolved, through cultivated conversation and through art prose, in a university atmosphere like that of Bologna. A most perfect model of this illustrious vulgar tongue was the language of Guido Cavalcanti, that of Cino da Pistoia, and his own. He believed that this language of the best Italian poets was a common language for the whole peninsula, that speech, to put it another way, which, eliminating all the localisms, best exemplified the true linguistic type peculiar to Italy.

Dante's mistake has its justification in the speculation of those times; it is a notable sign of the deep feeling of nationality that Dante possessed; this treatise provides the first clear expression of that feeling. For him "Italy" always means the entire peninsula and never merely that northern part of it which was, or had been, the actual "kingdom of Italy"; for him the "language of Italy" comprises all the dialects from the Alps to Sicily, and we sense a desire that all Italy be united under a single ruler just as she was already unified by her language and customs.* Moreover, the fact that Dante uses the terms *Italia* and *Latium, italus* and *latinus* or *latialis* indifferently, shows that the poet never thought of Italy without thinking of the head, Rome.

In the second book, he first shows that the "illustrious" vernacular tongue is used, not by all poets, but only by the

---
* *De Vulg.*, I, xvi, 3, and xviii, 5.

best; not for all subjects but only for the most elevated ones (deeds of war, love, virtue); not in all the metrical forms but only in the one that is most noble: the canzone. He then goes on to discuss the highest style, or as it was called, the "tragic" style, which alone is suitable to those three subjects; and establishes what kinds of verse, constructions, and words are most appropriate. Finally, he discusses the form and rules of the canzone; but the treatise breaks off just at the point where Dante starts speaking of the number of lines and syllables in the stanza

At the beginning of the treatise, Dante asserts the originality of his endeavor; it is in fact a real title of honor for him. The work is invaluable in many ways: it provides many details about the art of the versifier, but moreover (and this is of special importance), it tells us about the art of the poet of the *Divina Commedia*. It demonstrates, above all, how much Dante felt the necessity of art along with that of inspiration; art, for him, is study and knowledge and is acquired through assiduous devotion to great teachers.*·

The Epistles

In no other work do we find, as we do in the *Epistles,* so many traces of Dante's literary education and of the subjection of so original a mind to the pedantry of the school in the pursuit of an art that we would call artificial. The *Epistles* are written, of course, in Latin, even when the topic and the people to whom they are sent do not require it. They are composed according to the rigid rules of the *Artes dictandi:* it was a universally accepted canon that the ornate style was the only

---

* *Ibid.,* II, iv, 9–10.

mark distinguishing the learned from the unlearned, and the precepts of the *cursus* made prose the subject of no less intense a study than that expended upon verse. Critics have expressed, and continue to express, doubts about the authenticity of some of Dante's extant letters, but we have no valid reasons for denying that he was their author, except for one written in Italian to Guido da Polenta. The others, though composed in the ornamental style dictated by the rhetoric of the schools, reveal the thought, the moral convictions, the manner of Dante. Blind chance has saved three notes written in the name of the Countess of Battifolle to Margaret of Brabant, the wife of Henry VII. They are important only as evidence that Dante, during his exile, wrote many letters on behalf of others. We must greatly lament the loss of other letters addressed to the people of Florence and to individual citizens of the government. In these messages he mourned his unjust sentence and recalled the outstanding services he had rendered to the city and the Guelph party.

All in all, there are only ten letters left to us, not counting the three notes written for the Countess of Battifolle. One is addressed to the Cardinal of Ostia, legate of the Holy See in Tuscany, in the name of the council and the whole body of the White party; two letters accompany some verses of Dante to Cino da Pistoia and Moroello Malaspina; in another he mourns with Oberto and Guido, counts of Romena, the death of their uncle A(lessandro?) "romanae aulae palatinus in Tuscia." Most elevated in tone is the letter to a member of the Florentine clergy (*Amico Florentino*) in which he refuses the chance to return to his homeland by means of an oblation to St. John. Of great importance are the three letters which were composed on the occasion of the descent of the Emperor Henry into Italy, not only because they reveal the life of the exile in those days, but also because they are a record of the progressive development of Dante's political thought between the writing of the *Convivio* and the *Monarchia*. Two letters (as well as one of those written for the Countess of Battifolle) are dated from the years of "the most auspicious march into Italy of Henry the Caesar." In them he indicates that he would recognize the emperor only when he became in fact king of the Romans, governing Italy from Rome; he calls himself *italus* in the title of the letter *Universis et singulis Italiae regibus* etc., intending thus to speak as an Italian to the Italians of the whole peninsula. He urges all of them, from the peaks of the Alps to the shores of the sea which surrounds every part of the peninsula, to go to meet their king, the *rex Romanorum* whose dominion is the world, and who, by means of his good rule, will render them genuinely free of every tyrannical government.*

The style of these letters is noteworthy, for it shows Dante animated by a spirit of prophecy, by that spirit which manifests itself more openly in the *Commedia,* not only when he announces the Greyhound, but, in the wider Biblical sense, as an interpreter of the word of God and as a herald of His will. His age influences him a little, but this attitude stems mainly from Dante's faith which enabled him to perceive the divine will at work in the things of this world, and, through his feeling of being backed by the word of God, gave him the courage to advise, persuade, and threaten. He seemed a *vox clamantis in deserto.* His language may seem to superficial minds of our day to be inappropriate, or worse, that of a high-flown rhetorician; it was, on the contrary, the mode of expression demanded by his beliefs and by his fervor as a citizen and a Christian. In the emperor he beheld the anointed

---

* *Epist.,* V, 19: "Awake then all you inhabitants of Italy and arise before your king, since you are destined not only to obey his command, but, as free men, to follow his guidance."

of the Lord. To set oneself against his authority was to transgress "human and divine law,"* to make of the human race a "beast of many heads"† which wore itself out in vain endeavors and became lost in the pursuit of particular aims contrary to those willed by providence. Such a style seems more appropriate in the letter written to the Italian cardinals after the death of Clement V, the purpose of which is to exhort them to elect a pope who would reëstablish the seat of the papacy in Rome. As Jeremiah wept over the widowed Jerusalem, Dante weeps over the city of the new chosen people whom Christ himself had confirmed as rulers of the world. He mourns over the city which Peter and Paul had drenched with their blood and consecrated as the apostolic see. Dante visualizes Rome "now deprived of either light, an object to be pitied by Hannibal himself, to say nothing of others, sitting solitary and widowed." He is the least important of Christ's sheep, but the word of God was once uttered by the mouths of sucklings, and truth was confessed by a man born blind. What a shameful thing that among so many shepherds and in such a flock "there is only one voice, one pitiful and private voice, to be heard at the funeral, as it were, of Mother Church." His zeal impels him to speak; greatly perturbed, he urges the Italian cardinals to fight "for the bride of Christ, for the seat of the bride, which is Rome, for our Italy, and to speak more grandly, for the whole community of the pilgrims on earth." Do not allow the infamy of the Gascons, who still seek to usurp the glory of the Italians, to triumph.

The letter with which Dante sent some cantos of the *Paradiso* to Cangrande della Scala, including in it an explanation of the subject and aims of the entire *Commedia* and a commentary on the prologue of the third canticle, has often proved

---
* *Ibid.*, VI, 5.
† *Mon.*, I, xvi, 4.

a source of disappointment to Dante students. Perhaps their severe and obstinate insistence that this letter is spurious is due to their inability to find therein a confirmation of their own prejudices concerning the poem. We should be willing to relinquish the claim that Dante foresaw all our curiosity and our ambitious critical reconstructions; we should bear in mind that scholastic practice imposed rather rigorous limits upon even the freest minds in treating such a subject matter; furthermore, we should consider that what Dante was concerned with saying, and what we preferably seek in him, is openly expressed in the whole poem, and that it did not therefore occur to him to make an explicit statement of it in this general introduction which prefaces his work. Whoever considers all this will not let himself be so impressed by the subtle and quibbling arguments of contemporary critics (or rather of the critics of yesteryear) as to deny the authenticity of a letter which reveals the mind and style of Dante so clearly. The revelation, in fact, is so clear that little more is to be desired; it ranges all the way from the title, where he designates himself "florentinus natione, non moribus," to the precise commentary on the first tercets of the *Paradiso*.

De Monarchia

The *Monarchia* is the treatise which expounds Dante's political philosophy in the most orderly and complete fashion. The date of composition cannot be accurately ascertained, since the work contains no references to Dante's contemporaries or to actual political events of his time. We must entirely exclude the possibility that it might have been written while Dante was in Florence on the occasion of the jurisdictional quarrels with the papal court. We must further rule out the possibility that one part may have been written at that time and another part later, after the death of Henry VII; the treatise is too tightly knit in conception and execution to allow of this assumption. The work is surely later than the *Convivio* because what, in the latter, is merely an idea, is fully developed in the *Monarchia*. Certain assertions of the *Convivio*, which experience showed Dante to be imprudent, are sidestepped in the *Monarchia*, or are set forth only after the entire treatise renders their meaning clear. Most probably the composition of the *Monarchia* took place during the years of Henry's descent into Italy when opposition to Henry became stronger, and the success of the enterprise that had aroused so many hopes in the exiled poet seemed uncertain. Since it treats a learned subject, of more than Italian concern, the essay is naturally in Latin. It is divided into three parts. In the first book Dante proves that temporal monarchy is necessary for the well-being of the world; in the second, that the Roman people have rightly assumed the monarchic office; in the third, that the authority of the Roman monarch stems immediately from God and not from any minister or vicar of His.

Dante's boast that he is "expounding truths unattempted by others"* has been disputed. It has seemed to many that others had already maintained his doctrines. There is no doubt that this or that idea had already been affirmed in broad terms, and that all of his concepts had a tradition of their own which went back to the first centuries of the Middle Ages, and even further. But as a matter of fact, if we look carefully, we find that there was no book in which Dante would have found nothing to censure; none seemed to prove its case with arguments he would have considered the most valid. It does not matter very much that many of the poet's lines of reasoning

---

* *Ibid.*, I, i, 3.

seem to us to be of scant value. Dante is a man of the Middle Ages, and he tries to move his contemporaries with reasons that had the most authority at the time. There existed neither a sure apperception of legal reality nor a precise historical grasp of the development of medieval public institutions. With the greatest good will in the world, it would not have been possible to understand clearly the actual juridical status of this king of the Romans who was to be chosen by the German nation, but who did not become emperor unless he was anointed and crowned by the pope in Rome. He was announced as the lord of the whole world, but his authority was not even recognized in all the territories subject to his direct jurisdiction. The very capital of his Empire where he had to be consecrated before he could fulfill his official duties was outside his effective domain. Unless he went to Rome for his coronation with sufficient forces to secure compliance with his orders, he would have to pledge his oath, to confirm rights, including the very right which shut him out of the city from which he derived his title to the government of the world; the right which hindered him from administering even temporary justice there. But with these matters, those who debated the status of Empire and Church were little concerned. In their discussions they disregarded actual conditions and the real bases of law, perhaps because factual situations seemed to them to be temporary or abusive, or perhaps because the fundamentals of law were not well known and controversialists fastened only upon those statutes which could be of use to them. Thus, arguments of abstract reason as well as theological proofs and deductions prevailed over the arguments of law. Dante adds to them the testimony of his poets, especially Virgil; he sets great store by the miracles which, he claims, God performed in giving to the men of a small city the dominion of the world, and he exploits allegories and arguments drawn from Holy Writ. More than that: he emphasizes the special character of his argument against churchmen who relied more heavily upon the text of the Decretals than upon the word of God and the authority of the Holy Fathers. Here too, he sometimes assumes the attitude and tone already noticed in the *Epistles;* for him the matter is not simply a political question, but a question of the salvation of man. It is not a purely human concern for man's welfare, but a divine command. Everyone ought to refrain from opposing it, especially he who is the representative of Christ upon earth.

Experience and long thought had given Dante the certainty that the principal cause of the evils which ravaged Italy and the world was not so much the transfer of the Empire to the German nation (where the emperor, engrossed by the cares of his various kingdoms, might neglect his highest duties on the other side of the Alps) as it was the pope's usurpation of the office which God had assigned to the emperor. The transfer of the Empire to Germany was a transitory thing, but the papal usurpation hindered Caesar from fulfilling his mission. Since such usurpation was caused by greed for earthly goods, the Church had deviated from her proper function and through her bad example had become a fomenter of the lowest desires in the flock entrusted to her care. Some writers have maintained that the first and second books of this essay were written to oppose the French Guelphs who were trying to free their country from subjection to both the Empire and the court of Rome, and that the third book was written to withstand the policy of the papacy. Actually the whole treatise is directed against all those who, for one reason or another, do not recognize the legitimacy of the Roman monarchy and its direct derivation from God. If on the whole it tends to confute the claims of the Church, that is because the Church has more authority and there is more harm in her usurpations. Further,

Dante gives evidence, relative to the Church, of that restraint which is so fitting in everything, and of that sense of justice which he invokes in favor of the Empire. He acknowledges, according to the more generally accepted point of view prevailing in both the ecclesiastical and the legal tradition, that independence must not be understood in such a narrow sense "as that the Roman prince is not subordinate in anything to the Roman pontiff, since that mortal happiness is, in a certain sense, ordained with a direct bearing upon immortal happiness." On the contrary, the emperor must cherish for the pope "that reverence which a first-born son should display to his father, so that, illuminated by the light of a father's favor, he may, with greater efficacy, shed his light upon the world over which he has been set by Him alone who is ruler of all spiritual and temporal things."* Between the two highest authorities there should be coördination of plans and activities, so that the human race may pursue first its earthly and then its celestial happiness; but one office should not be subordinate to the other: he who chooses and confirms the emperor is God himself.†

The Empire does not exclude individual states, "for nations, kingdoms, and cities have their own special particularities which must each be regulated by different laws."‡ The emperor enacts the universal law, and the rulers and the cities ought to accept it "as the practical intellect, with an eye upon the operational conclusion, accepts from the speculative intellect the major proposition, and ranges below it the particular proposition which is specifically its own; and hence proceeds to the particular operation."§ It is improbable that Dante had a precise idea of how to put his ideal into practice, and we

---
* *Ibid.*, III, xvi, 17-18.
† *Ibid.*, III, xvi, 12-15.
‡ *Ibid.*, I, xiv, 5.
§ *Ibid.*, I, xiv, 7.

must move cautiously in making deductions beyond what he has expressed. To him it was enough to affirm the general principles, that only in universal monarchy is justice practicable and peace obtainable, that the emperor has authority in the temporal sphere over all rulers and commonwealths of the earth, and that his law must be enforced in every part of it. That in reality the Empire did not extend over all the world and was not everywhere acknowledged were chance factors which did not invalidate the necessary inferences from those principles. The situation of Christianity was the same as that of the Empire: the fact that the Empire was not everywhere recognized did not hinder Dante from thinking that one day what God had ordained would be accomplished, and that meanwhile both the Church and the Empire must be considered sacred and universal institutions.

In the *Monarchia* Dante has not noted in detail what the relations of the emperor and king of the Romans to the kingdoms and existing republics were to be. Neither does he state what degree of self-government these minor political organisms might enjoy under paramount imperial or royal rule, or in what way Italy would enjoy political unity in spite of the variety of her states, since she would certainly have to have her king and court in Rome, in the person of the emperor. But it was a legal reality, if not a fact, that the emperor had that more direct sovereignty over Italy which he had also over Germany, in virtue of being king of the two kingdoms; and this special royal office made Dante hope for a more effective government in all parts of the peninsula through justice and peace, when the office of the emperor and that of king of the Romans (that is, of Italy) might be effectively implemented.

With respect to Rome, there are more precise indications on the question whether or not Constantine had the right to grant the seat of the Empire to the Church. Dante denies that right absolutely and concedes only that the emperor could "allot a patrimony and other things for the protection of the Church, whereas the paramount dominion always remained intact, since its unity does not permit any division," and that the pontiff might "receive property, not in fee simple, but as dispenser of its fruits for the Church on behalf of the poor of Christ."* Hence his grief over the evil use that was made of Church revenues and ecclesiastical inheritances in his day: "They take no pity on the poor of Christ, whom not only do they cheat of the revenues of the churches, but the very patrimony of the Church herself is daily plundered; and she is pauperized, while they who make a show of justice, bar the admittance of the minister of justice." If this evil practice was to continue, it would be better that those patrimonies should return to their donors.† According to Dante, the fact that Rome was the imperial city need not hinder her from being simultaneously the seat of the Church: from the holy city, the Empire and the Church should look ahead, in perfect accord, to the happiness and salvation of humankind.

It has been said about Dante's political doctrines that they are utopian and a poet's dream, and they have been contrasted with the practical sense of the Florentines, stable, clear-sighted, and resolute in defending and increasing their own independence and the independence of all Italy from this authority exercised by barbarians. Doubtless the keen desire of the Florentines to insure the slow but sure attainment of self-government by the Italian communes is a marvelous thing. But the exiled Dante's point of view is not without justification either if we look back upon the political situation in an Italy, ravaged by wars and internecine struggles which made him liken her to "a ship without a pilot in a great

---

* *Ibid.*, III, x, 16–17.
† *Ibid.*, II, xii, 1–2.

storm." The pilot must be an authority superior to all, who would control the fluctuations of rancor and greed, and would reconcile conflicting interests impartially, acting as an arbiter between the battling cities and factions. To repulse the emperor was to alienate the guardian of justice and peace in and among the cities; his people were choosing, as it were, to be slaves of some form of tyranny, whether it were a princedom, an oligarchy, or a democracy, instead of aspiring to that liberty and security which every citizen of a well-ordered state possesses within the limits and within the protection of the law. The legal basis of the Empire was not a dream of Dante's; the Empire was generally recognized even by those very people who, because of their individual interests, opposed it; it was generally believed capable of enacting its rule over the individual states that did not recognize its authority, at least in Italy, which Dante had in mind above all. And in this confidence that the work of the emperor would suffice to heal the wounds of the peninsula, Dante did battle. But actually, his great love for Italy, his admiration for what the Roman people had done in the world, the view which his studies and reflections had given him of the history of mankind, arousing and ennobling his feelings and his faith, led him to believe that the mission of the Empire was a divine one, bound up with the ends assigned by God to man in this life and the other, and hence incapable of defeat, however slow, however combatted in its progress. At any rate, it is not important for us to weigh Dante's political judgment; more pertinent is it to know what most kindled his emotions and inflamed his imagination. If it was a utopia, it was certainly a noble one. In espousing it, he did not show any less love for Italy and for her well-being and glory than did his more practical compatriots. By exalting and defending the Empire he exalted and defended an Italian glory. Even if historical contingencies or divine justice had temporarily granted the imperial crown to foreign rulers, they were still imperial rulers. The Empire was Roman in every way, and Rome had to be the seat of it; and Italy, "queen of the peoples," (*domina gentium*), thus had the honor of ruling the world.

The Eclogues

While Dante was bent upon completing his great poem during the peaceful days in Ravenna, toward the end of 1319, he received from Giovanni del Virgilio, teacher of Latin at nearby Bologna, a "song" which expressed displeasure that the venerable old poet should waste the treasure of his art upon the common people. Giovanni went on to say that he wanted Dante to celebrate one of the more important events of his time in the language of the classics, so that he might gain from the learned the title of poet laureate. Dante was pleased with the affection that the poem showed, and he answered with a Latin eclogue of felicitous inspiration, composed with an art which, for those times, was exquisite. He does not conceal his desire for the poet's laurel, but he expects it from the *Commedia*. He is hoping to receive the laurel crown in Florence whenever the *Paradiso* is finished and circulated like the other two canticles. Meanwhile he will send Giovanni ten cantos of the canticle he is composing, with the idea that they will settle the matter by removing the last scruples of the Bolognese teacher. Giovanni had reason to be excited by the answer of the new Tityrus and the precious gift: how could he not think that Dante was a revived Virgil? He wrote:

> O si quando sacros iterum flavescere canos
> fonte tuo videas et ab ipsa Phillide pexos,
> quam visando tuas tegetes miraberis uvas!⁸

But until the times are satisfactory, why will not Tityrus come to Bologna where they will be able to sing together, even if each in a different voice, and he will receive the crown from both young and old, all desirous of admiring the new songs and of learning the old ones? Dante replied with a second eclogue: the insistent invitation has frightened the friends of Tityrus who fear that they will be abandoned; he would like to please Mopsus, his gentle petitioner and correspondent, but he fears the dangers which, his friends tell him, may be in store for him in Bologna.

The two eclogues are of singular importance not only because they reveal much about Dante's life at Ravenna, his feelings, his hopes for the *Commedia;* but because they confirm so clearly what training he had had in the Latin poets before trying his new art, and prove what a help that training had been to him.

Quaestio de aqua et terra

For a long time critics have been uncertain about the authenticity of this essay, but they have finally decided to consider it genuine. Its topic was the subject of lively disputes in the schools and among writers: is water in its sphere or in its natural circumference, in any place, higher than the land which emerges from the waters, and which is commonly called the "habitable fourth?" It is not strange that Dante, who was, and professed himself to be, the servant of philosophy (*viro philosophiae domestico*), should somehow become involved in the controversy. Nor is it strange that because of his reputation as a philosopher he should be induced to discuss the question publicly and later to write out his argument; nor that he should obtain from the bishop of Verona (because of the traditional authority which bishops had over teaching) the right to debate the matter, in a small chapel in the city where he was well known and admired for his knowledge and ranked as a gentleman, even though he had not taken a doctor's degree.

Having listed the five arguments adduced by the upholders of the theory that water is higher, he demonstrates in the first part of his rebuttal that it is impossible for water to be anywhere higher than the emergent land; in the second, he proves that the emergent land is at every point higher than the entire surface of the sea; in the third, he lists and rejects the objections put forward by the opponents of what he has demonstrated thus far; in the fourth, he attempts to trace the final and efficient cause of the emergence of the land, in the form of a half moon or thereabouts; in the fifth, he concludes by disposing of the five arguments adduced in the beginning against the truth demonstrated by him.

At one time great importance was attached to this dissertation because of the nine cosmological truths confirmed by modern science which Dante supposedly foretold and in part demonstrated in it. Although it has been asserted that this was the result of a too credulous criticism and that Dante's knowledge in these matters did not surpass that of his age, the *Quaestio* remains a considerable testimony of Dante's love for the truth, in which he declared himself "continuously nurtured" (*continue nutritus*) from his childhood, and of the sure knowledge that he had at the command of his poetic imagination when he came to construct his otherworldly kingdoms.

Part III
The Divine Comedy

Genesis and Composition

The earliest idea of what was Dante's greatest work stems doubtless from the plan to exalt Beatrice. The *Vita Nuova* ends with this promise: "There appeared to me a wonderful vision wherein I saw things which made me determine to say nothing more of this blessed one until I could more worthily speak of her; and for this reason I study all I can, as she truly knows. Wherefore, if it be His pleasure, in whom all things live, that my life endure a few more years, I hope to say of her what has never been said before of any woman."

It is useless to conjecture what he intended to do at that time and to ask whether anything might actually have been written with that plan in mind. He could not, however, forget so solemn a promise, not even in those years during which studies, politics, and the first worries of exile demanded his whole attention. When the plan was actually revived in his mind and to what years the composition of the poem may be traced are two questions which have been long and subtly discussed. Some writers, admitting that Dante had been thinking for some time of the *Commedia* and was steadily preparing the subject matter of it, maintain that he did not begin its composition until after the death of Henry VII. According to others, however, composition may have been started about the year 1307; so that the first two canticles were probably finished before the death of Henry or shortly after, and only the *Paradiso* occupied the last years of the poet's life. This second opinion seems more probable; we have sure proof that before April, 1314, it was already possible to speak of a work "quod dicitur Comedia, et de infernalibus inter cetera multa tractat," as of a work, in part at least, generally known and therefore published. There are other indications; and, moreover, Dante himself, in the first eclogue,* attests that, before the *Paradiso* was completed, the other two canticles had already been circulated. ("Quum mundi circumflua corpora cantu / astricolaeque meo, velut infera regna, patebunt.")[1] This makes it very likely that the *Inferno* and the *Purgatorio* had been published, if not together, at least only a brief time apart, shortly after the death of Henry. It may actually be that in 1306, while he was at the court of the Malaspina family, he received from Florence parts of a work that he had written there in praise of Beatrice. It may also be that the hard experience of exile forewarned him of the scant effect that a purely doctrinal treatise might have in healing the wounds of Italy. Perhaps his poetic nature, constrained and mortified by the hard discipline of philosophy and learning, regained, at a certain moment, the upper hand. It is probable that toward the year 1307 the idea of a work in verse came with the force of sheer necessity to his mind; a work which, over many years, had hauntingly whirled round and round in his spirit; a poem that would give expression to his memories, desires, experiences, ideas, hopes. In it he would attempt to reform humanity and particularly Italy, which was steadily moving away from the ideal of a truly political and Christian life.

Just as Aeneas had been destined by divine providence to prepare the birth of Rome and her universal Empire, and the apostle Paul had been chosen to spread the Christian Faith among the peoples, so Dante, afire with the idea of his great

---

* *Ecl.*, I, 48–49. "When the wheeling planets of the universe and the dwellers of the stars shall be shown forth, as are already the lower kingdoms, in my song..."

poem, will feel himself called upon to show the ravages brought about by the lack of the two guides appointed by God for the welfare of men, and to prophesy divine aid so that the divine plan may be restored. Civil honors, the care of earthly goods, shall revert to the Empire; the Church, free of duties which are not hers, shall resume the mission for which she was founded, shall guide men to heaven opened again to them by the sacrifice of Christ. Meanwhile he will present himself as an example of a man who returns to the truly religious life after recognizing the vanity of earthly goods. With the disappearance of the woman who had guided him "upon the right path" to love, the highest good, he became engrossed by temporal matters and started to travel down the road to perdition; but being a devout son of Mary, a loyal friend of justice, and a friend of Beatrice, he was not to die. The visit to the three realms of the other world under the guidance of Virgil sent by Beatrice, the guidance of Beatrice herself, the year of the great jubilee of 1300, all these shall make his soul whole again and render him worthy to reveal what God has arranged for the salvation of all mankind. Thus the plan of the poem born in exile, directed to a nobly social and religious end, is joined with the early idea of a work in which the poet would say of Beatrice what had never been said of any other woman.

It is not possible to trace the history of the composition of the poem in its successive phases during the ten and more years that it went on. The critics who have tried to do so, in their desire to be exact, have fallen into subtle and arbitrary conjectures. The beginnings were perhaps more modest than the whole poem indicates. Although the style was from the very outset what might be expected in a work that was to be called a *Commedia,* with its meter derived from the popular *serventese,* little by little Dante's artistic conscience made him feel that he could enter into competition with the great Latin poets.* His inspiration became progressively more elevated in tone, more consciously artistic,† until what was at first a "comedy" became a "sacred poem" for which neither the middle style nor the most common language sufficed; its style itself led to an early division of the work into three parts; and the numbers "three" and "ten" (two numbers of special significance for Dante, one as a symbol of the Trinity, the other as the symbol of perfection, according to the ideas of the age) became the regulating principle of the moral architecture of the three kingdoms, both in that first embryonic structure which is indispensable for every conception, poetic or otherwise, and in that successive elaboration of ideas and creation with which inspiration finally reaches its destined form. Thus we find three canticles for the three otherworldly realms, Inferno, Purgatory, Paradise; each canticle in thirty-three cantos, with one canto as an introduction to the entire poem, totaling exactly one hundred, multiple of ten. The Inferno, a vast abyss in the center of the earth, is divided into nine circles, plus the vestibule; there are as many divisions for the realm of purgation, a high mountain which rises from the midst of the ocean in the southern hemisphere, with the terrestrial Paradise at its peak; nine heavens, according to the Ptolemaic system, plus the empyrean, constitute Paradise. The sinners are arranged in the Inferno according as their sin stems from incontinence, violence, or fraud. The penitents in Purgatory are distributed according to whether their love is directed toward evil, or if directed toward good, with too much or too little zeal. The spirits of Paradise are divided into *sæculares, activi,* and *contemplativi,* according to whether their worldly passions perturbed their love of God, or whether this love ex-

---
* *Inf.,* XXV, 94–102.
† *Purg.,* IX, 70–72.

pressed itself in the active or the contemplative life. The metrical device is the chain-linked tercet. As soon as the inspiration found its form, the whole was planned with consummate precision. The three canticles have almost the same number of lines,* and each canticle ends with the word "stars." Such facts are external, but noteworthy, evidence of a most felicitous and powerful genius that could combine the most sublime and burning inspiration with rigorous meditation and minute craftsmanship of form.

Inferno

In his treatment of the Inferno, it hardly seems necessary to say, Dante has not broken completely with the classical tradition of poetry, and in particular with Virgil. The novelty of his poem was to consist not in the substitution of hitherto untreated material for a familiar world, material which could very easily be fitted to new needs and a new creation, but rather in what would be depicted within that world. The Christian religion had already transformed the gods and monsters of pagan myth into demons; Dante more boldly mingles the Biblical and the mythological traditions and gives the appearance of newness to everything. Thus we find the rivers Acheron, Styx, Phlegethon, and Cocytus in his Inferno, but Lethe is more suitably transported to the peak of Purgatory. Catholic thought in Dante's time gave demons the role of tormenting the damned and of presiding over Hell; thus we find Minos, Charon, Cerberus, Plutus, Phlegyas, the Furies, Medusa, and other monsters of classical tradition carrying out one or the other of these offices. Among them we meet the

---

* *Ibid.*, XXXIII, 139–141.

Minotaur, the Centaurs, the Harpies, Geryon; and along with them, the devils of Biblical tradition in their customary forms, or as dogs, serpents, or dragons. Lucifer himself is among them, entrusted with the direct punishment of the betrayer of Christ, the founder of the Church, and of the betrayers of Caesar, the founder of the Empire. But since all these creatures could not be left out of the poem because religious faith looked upon them as real beings, necessitating their relegation to the Inferno, and since they were already too well known in the arts, they are here introduced as ornament and structural detail, rather than as the essentially poetical part. The *Commedia* derives its poetry from actual beings, famous in ancient and contemporary history, and from Dante himself, a living man who goes among them to awaken their memories and to stir up their passions anew.

Dante labors to make us feel the horror of that kingdom of darkness and grief and his own fear and anxiety during this extraordinary, superhuman journey. Not even here, however, do we feel that powerful response which is usually called forth by the vague grandeurs of poetry. The poet must come in contact with other spirits in order to produce genuine poetry. We find now an uncontrollable pity for the passions which confound frail human nature; now a deeper perturbation before the errors and weaknesses of admired compatriots, beloved teachers, noble spirits of every age, now a burning sympathy for beings whose good works did not save them from ungratefulness and persecution. At other times, we meet with Dante's outbursts of indignation, both as a man and as a citizen, against sinners bereft of all goodness and sullied with sins that disgust the conscience of every decent man.

Since the prevailing emotion among the spirits must be despair, this is the first thing noticed by the poet as he enters the gate of Hell. The presence of a living man among the lost spirits, sufficient to make them forget their tortures for a moment, carries them away into the world of memories, rekindles in them the turbulent emotions of their former life. Hence, at every meeting, a different outburst of emotions, a new depiction of human affairs takes place. These episodes acquire vividness by being projected to us from a world so faraway and so mysterious, by being compared with the sentiments in the soul of Dante, inclined on the one hand to esteem courtesy, valor, and all the virtues and aspirations which ennoble human nature, and on the other, embittered by exile, consumed by a burning and perhaps foolish desire for righteousness and justice, full of anxiety about the fate of Italy and humanity, both of them abandoned to the fury of passion and covetousness.

He does not always linger over the sin which has brought the spirits to Hell; on the contrary he often prefers to re-evoke what has nothing to do with their damnation, as with Farinata, Brunetto, or Ulysses, or what may arouse a human response; for example, not the act of betrayal performed and suffered by Count Ugolino, but the cruel mode of his death. From time to time he is greatly moved by his memory of what is happening throughout Italy when he has to recount it in order to satisfy the desire of the anxious shades for news of matters and persons dear to them. Then the spirits and the poet are like exiles in a far-off land who move one another to tenderness by speaking of their country.* Nor are all the spirits portrayed in that attitude of impenitence, which would render them theologically perfect as damned souls, but poetically less vivid. In many of them there remains all the variety of emotions which might be found in living sinners; thus Capaneus and Vanni Fucci are obstinate in their impiety, Francesca attempts to justify her love as inevitable, Pier della

---

* Cf. *Inf.*, X, 26; XVI, 58; XXVII, 37.

Vigna acknowledges the weakness which made him, though just, unjust with himself, and Guido da Montefeltro mourns because he did not know how to persevere in penitence.*

Owing to the great variety of inspirations, we have in the Inferno a series of episodes (Francesca, Farinata, Pier della Vigna, Ulysses, Count Ugolino, and others) of such poetical power as to outweigh the other two canticles on this score. There are scenes of marvelous movement mixed in with the portrayal of vigorous characters, like that of the demons in Malebolge, sometimes fully drawn, sometimes merely sketched with a few broad strokes. The account gradually takes on the tone and color suitable to each rank of sinners; even vulgar scenes, gestures, and allusions are cleverly, boldly employed, wherever appropriate, in order to make this first kingdom of the other world beyond the grave more varied and more vivid.

Purgatorio

If the Inferno is the kingdom of shadows and despair, with its plaints and curses, hatred and deceit, where even Dante thinks it a courtesy to be rude, Purgatory is the kingdom of open and clear air, of harmony, peace, and hope. Here is that harmony of wills which are no longer divided in the pursuit of earthly goods, but united in the acquisition of that good which does not wane, but rather increases, the more there are to share it.† Here is that peace which is God's pardon and which inclines the spirits to forgive whoever has been unjust to them; it makes them sorrowful both for the evil they have

---
* *Ibid.,* XXVII, 84.
† *Purg.,* XV, 46-81.

committed and for the evil they see committed by others. Here is that hope of mounting soon to God, and in this hope their pain becomes a comfort.

The "dead poesy" of the first canticle here seems to become serene, like the soul of Dante, as it issues forth from darkness to the "gentle blue of orient sapphire" that brightens the wide and tranquil horizon of this realm. From the time of his unexpected arrival under the starry heaven in the hour when the star of Venus gives promise of the approaching dawn until, with the sun on his brow, he arrives among the "great variety of tender blossoms" of the terrestrial Paradise, everything is brought into musical accord with the new state of souls, with the new emotions of the poet. Casella sings on the island's shore surrounded by the infinite sea, and so sweetly that the spirits most anxious for their purgation, and Virgil himself, stop to listen to him as if "their minds heeded nothing else." The spirits also sing, invoking grace on their atonement and rejoicing for those who, finally purified, leave the mountain to rise to the glory of Paradise. Matilda sings like a woman in love while she weaves garlands out of the flowers with which her path is colored.

Viewed in the setting of the poem as a whole the *Purgatorio* may be called the canticle of combined tenderness and melancholy. There is no invective except on the part of the narrator who grows indignant when he compares what he has seen there with earthly reality. Rather, there is lamentation, sorrowful wonderment, passionate resentment that is intensified by the general moderation of the spirits being purified, and thrown into relief by the entire atmosphere of forgiveness. This we see in the princes of the valley, in Rinieri da Calboli, Marco Lombardo, Hugh Capet, and Forese Donati. Only in the terrestrial Paradise do such outbursts of reproof and indignation, which break out here and there as though under compulsion, seem to be concentrated and developed. They occur first in the reproaches of Beatrice to Dante, and then in the prediction of the vengeance of God against those who have corrupted the Church and ruined the divine plan for world order. Here even Beatrice takes part, "sighing and compassionate," in the procession symbolizing that corruption; and if her pity for Dante seems "harsh," it is always the pity of a mother who has wept much for the sins of her favored son.

The *Purgatorio* also contains a great variety of figures and scenes, from Cato and Manfred to Arnaut Daniel and Matilda, from the disembarking of the new spirits to be purified on the bank of the island to the allegorical representation of the earthly Paradise. It is true that none of these is as dramatic as those in the *Inferno* owing to the very nature of this kingdom, where the spirits no longer live in their sin as a still present and perturbing passion, but aspire instead with all their ardor to an entirely different life. Nevertheless the poetry does not flow less clearly from their memories and hopes than from their passions; only it is more intimate and full of tender pathos. The poet himself, as though stimulated by the beauty of the place, delights in recreating that world of art for which he was especially molded by nature and in re-evoking the memories of his happier years. How many artists there are in this second canticle: Casella, Belacqua, Sordello, Oderisi, Statius, Bonagiunta, Guido Guinizelli, and Arnaut Daniel. What long discourses are held between Virgil and Statius about art and the creatures they have immortalized, while Dante follows them, listening to the conversations which give him "an intellectual understanding of poetry." We might say that Purgatory itself wishes to contribute to the glory of art, presenting, in one of its circles, a new kind of art beyond ordinary human skill which the astonished poet tries to describe in words: the bas-reliefs, which were a "speech made visible," and whilst seen in profile, "the dead seemed dead and the living seemed alive."

In no other canticle are the emotions so sweetly expressed. Here the spirits are not so perpetually engrossed in their atonement and so eager to hasten their union with God that no room is left for the outbreak of earthly emotions. Those whom Dante sees approaching allow themselves to be enticed by the song of Casella "as though forgetting to go and endue themselves with beauty." At the sight of a living man, Conrad Malaspina does not have eyes, that night, for the serpent tempter. Even Statius, in the final act of mounting wholly purified to heaven, would consent to postpone the blessed vision of God another year for the sight of Virgil.

Paradiso

Paradiso is, above all, the canticle of Beatrice. That a blessed creature should watch with particular care over the welfare of individual men who live the hard and dangerous life of the world is a common idea of the Middle Ages; but for the poet to have chosen Beatrice for this role is a novelty which injects a beautiful note of humanity and love into the third canticle. It is entirely right and good that Virgil, whom Dante calls "my dearest father" and "my more than father," should give way to Beatrice, his "sweet and dear guide" who lived "in heaven with the angels" and once had lived "on earth with his soul"; Dante, thus, had good reason to call her "his lady." During his journey through the celestial spheres he depends upon her shining eyes, those eyes which had had the power to move Virgil to immediate help. Her smile, which becomes progressively more joyful, is a sign of the gradual ascent from the lower heavens toward the seat of divinity. It is she who foresees all things, arranges all things, and gives satisfaction in all things.

There are scholars who scoff at what may be called the "theological" Beatrice; they maintain that she is a product of a cold imagination. But their idea stems from an unimaginative, prejudiced attempt to reconstruct Dante's vision. Beatrice enlightens Dante at the proper time and place without putting on a great show of intellect. She is a saint and thus speaks of things that every saint naturally knows in the continuous vision of God. Nor does she perform only the function of informing Dante about the new things that appear to his sight and of clarifying the doubts that arise in his mind. With the affection and the solicitude of a mother or an older sister she instructs and admonishes him in those things which she thinks may prove useful to him here in our blind world. She is happy that God has granted such grace to her faithful one, and that He has given her the privilege of guiding Dante to the Empyrean. The charity that animates all the blessed, and which is an indication and increase of their blessedness, does the rest.

Not only in Beatrice's sweet eyes "is Paradise," as she herself warns. Through the felicitously imagined appearances of the souls in their various heavens, according to the influences felt by them in life, Dante finds himself in contact with those spirits whom he most loved and admired and whom he therefore most desired to see in glory; these he wished to describe, with these he wished to speak. As in the other kingdoms, here too the human appearance remains, a token anticipating the resurrection of the flesh; and if it is no longer possible to recognize the real appearances of the denizens of Paradise in the increasing light above the lower heavens, the emotions of

THE DIVINE COMEDY *81*

the blessed are shown by indirect means which permit our imaginations constantly to coöperate with the art of the poet and to give to the poet's vision that indeterminate quality which is most suitable to the depiction of the divine.

On close inspection, the third canticle is not essentially different from the others. Paradise, for Dante, is not a pure union of the soul with its creator. The blessed were once men, and although their happiness is in God and their wills are stably centered in Him, nothing hinders them from loving and remembering what was once their world and from taking an interest in the Church militant, that is, in their fellow men who still live the earthly life. Dante is a pilgrim who has received from God the special grace of partaking of supernal happiness "before his soldier's service has been completed" and of knowing secrets hidden from mortal eyes. He nevertheless brings with him his doubts and desires, his passions and hopes, and he kindles passions and hopes in these blessed spirits; he prays, sings, becomes wrathful and exalted with them. He has with him as his faithful follower the memory of those left behind on earth who are desirous to know the life that awaits them after death, or the fate that providence has decreed for this world, a world which, through the fault of those who should guide it toward the good, seems each day more inclined toward ruin.

In brief, not even in Paradise does Dante portray things of pure imagination outside the reality in which we live and in which we love and suffer and hope. To that other world he transports this world of ours, not only its present, but its past which lives in our memories and in our emotions, and its future which lives in our hopes: God and man, intellect and feeling, religion and politics, theology and philosophy, science and art, everything that enlists the interest of man, everything for which daily he wears himself out in speculation and work, and by which he is distressed and elated. And if poetry is not merely a representation of sensuous nature or of the most common sentiments, but also of the fire of profound truth, it cannot be said that the poetry of the *Paradiso* is weak or played out. The speculations of Dante are not merely the frigid elucubrations of a professional philosopher or theologian: he speculates because he feels the need of explaining what is around him; he must find bases for what he believes, hopes, and does. From effects he rises to causes, up to the first cause; but from God he returns to God's creatures with a more intense attachment, as if from the most elevated and profound contemplations, from the purging of his emotions he emerged more alive and felt it more incumbent upon him to express his affection for his fellow beings created in the image of God, and for the entire creation in which the shadow of the Eternal Worth is manifested. He feels all the dignity of man even within the limits imposed upon reason and within the *vulneratio* of his nature as a result of the primal sin; and in the struggle of our free will he recognizes our real virtue. The poem itself, over which daily he has grown "lean," is conceived as a battle, his last great battle; and it is precisely in the *Paradiso* that the serious problems connected with the divine governance of the world undergo their broadest and most solemn development. Here we have the apotheosis of the Roman Empire willed by God for the peace of the world and for the development of human civilization; here the exaltation of justice as the sovereign virtue in the governments of the world; here the glorification of those who, with pure intentions, labor in the search for truth in human and divine knowledge, the extolment of those who work nobly and die for the Faith, of those who, by the example of a truly religious life, invite and encourage us to the real reverence that is owed to God and to the detachment of ourselves from the cares and greeds of the world that have corrupted the shepherds and their Christian flocks along with them. And here, amidst this widespread concern of the blessed with the world's corruption, Dante, the poor exiled friend of justice, is solemnly entrusted with the mission of revealing to the world the truth that the Pharisees abuse or adulterate, and of announcing that divine assistance is at hand.

It is natural that here and there in the fabric of Paradise some element of mysticism should appear; it develops spontaneously from the inmost core of the action. What can human knowledge, what can the terrestrial life mean to these saints, to Dante himself, a witness and participant in that happiness of theirs? But after giving himself up briefly to it, the human side in him revives; in short, the *Paradiso* is more than the glorification of the divine in itself; it is a celebration of the divine in its effects, a statement in lyric yet epic terms of the highest achievements of humanity.

The Poetic Unity of the Commedia

Dante intended to create a poem, not in our modern fashion, but rather according to the ideas of his age which concurred in conceiving of a poetry that did not exclude the practical ends of teaching and moral reform. Our own notions are perhaps more correct: we discriminate between those places in the *Commedia* where such poetry predominates, expands, and triumphs, and passages which to our minds are pure rhetoric, conceptual abstractions, or simply structure. According to Dante, his great work was wholly poetry, owing to the right employment of diction and figures and the use of meter; and the more or less poetical diversity of tone did not lead to disharmony among the various parts, since the whole was inspired and animated by a single emotion that gripped the spirit of the poet for more than ten years in a state of ecstatic exaltation and excitement. The entire poem has the timbre, the coloring, the accent which we now call Dantean.

We need not think that because of the practical ends of the work the writer found it necessary at first to make a kind of outline, availing himself of cold reason and erudition in place of imagination and inspiration, and that only after having constructed his massive castle did he think of the adornments. Once Dante had the idea that nothing was more suited to his artistic and practical purposes than a depiction of the other world, he quickly made his first plan and began creation without worrying about whether he should or should not portray his innermost thoughts by following the inspiration of the moment, or whether the impulse that moved him was poetical or otherwise. His initial conception gave him great liberty, and he took advantage of it in order to satisfy all his needs and desires, whichever happened to prevail at the time. He abandoned himself to the creative impulse whenever his imagination carried him away; he yielded to his love for order and clarity whenever the subject matter, which was infinitely varied and unusual, demanded it; he inveighed and perorated whenever feeling kindled his soul; he discussed subtle questions of physics and metaphysics whenever the torment and anxiety of doubt, or the prospect of clarifying the subject excited and moved him. It is true that he lingers over certain figures, phrases, or discussions longer than our taste admits of. He lingers over them because of certain ideas or preconceptions about art, because of notions that he held as a poet of righteousness or as a learned man, owing to his "greedy" genius for learning. The power of a mind that organizes, orders, and supervises all makes itself felt everywhere. These facts are to be conceded; but it would be difficult to prove that the entire work fails to maintain a central force of inspiration that penetrates, with the same vital light, every point of the poem with more or less intensity, and makes us realize that the soul of Dante is at every moment in active control. From the very beginning his poetic genius has taken hold of the direction of the work uninterruptedly, and the whole has come gradually into being in spontaneous bursts from the heart of the subject, as Dante lived it.

The allegory does not turn out to be as fatal to the poem as certain critics imagine. Aside from the allegories which Dante himself has caused us to believe by his statement of them in the letter to Cangrande, or those contrived by the subtle minds of his interpreters, there is indeed an allegory present in the primitive conception of the poem; but it is one so general, so unobtrusive, that it has by no means impeded or cluttered the detailed composition that followed. We are referring to that meaning, parallel to the literal action, by which the journey of humanity toward earthly and heavenly bliss under the guidance of the Empire and the Church corresponds to the journey of Dante from the dark wood to the terrestrial Paradise under the leadership of Virgil, and to his ascent through the heavens under the guidance of Beatrice. The happy quality of his poetic genius led Dante to choose such personages for his depictions as to justify, even in the literal sense, what is subservient to the requirements of allegory. Therefore, in reading, we are not obliged to think of a meaning beyond that of the letter in order to enjoy the poem; and if we have been prepared to seek a fuller sense, that is a task we assume for our own greater satisfaction. Virgil is already, in himself, a spirit who "knew all"; he had been the singer of the Empire and the herald of the "new order"; Beatrice is a blessed spirit to whom everything is revealed through her contemplation of God; on earth she had already inclined Dante "to love that good beyond which is nothing that one may aspire to." The result is that everything they do in the poem, even in the allegorical meaning, is done with such naturalness and consistency that we can always follow the poet without either effort or difficulty.

The portrayal of the dark wood is different. Here, however, we do not have what is properly an allegory, but rather an extended metaphor which has the double function, first, of giving the poet a starting point for the figment of his journey through the eternal regions, and second, of bestowing significance upon that moral bewilderment which makes his journey necessary. If he, later, alludes to this moral bewilderment in various turns of phrase,* no disturbance in the coherence of the poetic representation results. We follow the writer without difficulty, as his poetic imagination leads us; in much the same way we ourselves continually mix, in our daily speech, metaphorical with literal expressions. If some interpreters of Dante's poem, not content with the light touch of its creator and the obvious meaning of his words, have complicated matters, we should not pay much attention to them. Thus certain symbolic figures scattered throughout the poem, like the Furies, the Old Man of Crete, Geryon, Cato, the Serpents, may provide no end of trouble for the subtlety of commentators; but to the wise, is not what the poet expressly says sufficient to make the deepest meanings of those figures clear?

As for the more complex configurations which we find in the terrestrial Paradise, we must consider the importance, in the progress of the poem, of the descent of Beatrice, since the exaltation of Beatrice is the dominating sentiment in the whole composition. We must consider the poetic necessity of arousing an appropriate expectation of so solemn an event.

---

* *Inf.*, XV, 50; *Purg.*, XXIII, 118; *Purg.*, XXVI, 58.

Certainly the figures of the terrestrial Paradise are all prepared with the purpose of using them to form a symbolic prophecy; but meanwhile the art of the poet leads us in the most natural way to the very threshold of such symbolic portrayal. The portrayal, then, proceeds so obviously and so rapidly, and is so tied in with the mission assigned to Dante by God or with the composition of the poem in the strictly literal sense, and furthermore so justified by God's wish that the poet should, by that vision, apprehend His will and proclaim it to mankind, that the reader could not wish for or imagine an episode more harmoniously and more closely bound up with the rest of the poem. And if anyone should seriously advance the charge of obscurity, Dante would be the first to be amazed by it. It is true, rather, that Beatrice does not have to explain any detail of the entire vision to her faithful charge. She merely says to him: "Have you seen? Carry your vision back as a warning to the misguided world." Can there be any uncertainty about the meaning of the griffin, the chariot, the eagle, the tree, or the vicissitudes of the chariot, if we remember Dante's history and ideas, instead of clinging to our own preconceived notions? It is more important for us to realize that the *Commedia* was not conceived, as is often affirmed, as an allegorical poem, but instead, as a revelation; and that the journey which it describes was not imagined so that Dante might spin out gossamers of subtle ideas, but so that he might announce what God had wanted him to see and hear in his "fateful passage," for the purpose of saving misguided humanity. Hence the importance of the literal meaning in the *Commedia*, and the great role that pure poetry plays in its doctrines and its practical ends.

Dante's World View

We will struggle in vain to find the internal unity of the work and to see everything in the right light if we fail to reproduce in our own selves, even down to the most minute particulars, the vision in which Dante lived for so many years with matchless intensity. Change followed upon change, his soul underwent many shocks, but his faith remained unshaken. Here and there in the poem we are able to discern a greater zeal, a more immediate hope; in some parts of it we even get the impression of more sharply outlined concepts as political developments gave him opportunities for more resolute affirmations. Nevertheless, his vision remains fundamentally the same; and even if the stormy vicissitudes of those years may have forced him to make some retouchings or additions, no trace of them is perceptible to the extent of impairing the internal unity of the great poem. The *Commedia* is entirely inspired by convictions and feelings that, by that time, have become the very life of its author.

Dante's firm belief, as a true Christian, is that man is a being created for the life to come; hence his inferences that the sin of Adam and the redemption achieved by Christ are the two most momentous facts in the history of mankind. Hence, also, the importance which the problems associated with the attainment of eternal happiness assume, beginning with the one that still torments the modern conscience, that is, the salvation of infidels. But Dante is not an ascetic, and not all his thought and emotions are wrapped up in a consideration of this otherworldly goal. He also recognizes that man, as a corruptible being, has an aim of his own on this earth; but, contrary to the Augustinian view, Dante contends that by this aim man is elevated and ennobled. Through his doctrine of

Empire, such a goal receives a more resolute and a broader affirmation than in St. Thomas. Even before divine grace opened the way to redemption, the human creature, corrupted by sin and born in sorrow, had been able by virtue of his reason (a pure gift of God) to live his life in a manner praiseworthy and meritorious in itself and in the sight of his Maker.* The fact that man's communal life may have evolved through violence and as a consequence of sin never appears in Dante's thought; the social impulse is a natural force toward the good, it is the counsel of reason that indicates the means of avoiding the evils deriving from sin. But the successive establishment of the family, the community, the city, and royal rule does not suffice for earthly happiness; through unbridled appetites the *politiae obliquae* (oligarchies, democracies, tyrannies) are soon born; and in order to bring about peace and perfect justice it becomes necessary to institute such a monarch "as, possessing everything, and therefore being unable to desire more, shall keep the kings content within the boundaries of their kingdoms, so that peace shall abide among them, wherein the cities may repose, and in this repose the neighborhoods may love one another, and in this love the families may satisfy all their needs. When this is accomplished, man may live happily."† Universal monarchy, however, is a thing that man could not attain by himself. Vain attempts were repeatedly made; but since man must, in sorrow, conquer that perfection and earthly happiness for which he was created, God intervened in his behalf. An additional motive for this intervention was that universal monarchy was providentially calculated to assist man's efforts toward redemption. For such an office God chose the Roman people, who were by nature the best disposed to it. And here, alongside the

---

* *Inf.*, IV, 78: "... [man's intellect] acquires Grace in heaven which thus advances him."

† *Conv.*, IV, iv, 4.

divine plan of redemption, we have the divine plan of Empire; here are the two *remedia* for the havoc wrought by the first sin, the two guides which lead to the two forms of happiness, one on the road which men travel, and the other on the road of God.

We must consider that the consequences of original sin still exist, and will continue to exist in human nature, notwithstanding the establishment of civil life and the redemption, even if the individual is able to escape those consequences through will and grace; a ruler who will guide humanity is therefore necessary. Just as the redemption did not restore human nature to the perfection of original justice but nevertheless gave man the means of saving himself, so the Empire, by securing justice and peace to the world, afforded the means of rendering effectual the sum of all available intelligence and of regaining, within the natural bounds wherein man is content,* that earthly happiness which was lost through the primal sin. It was for this reason that the Empire was founded, and not because it was actually necessary for redemption (as some, in Dante's time, believed). Two offices, distinct and independent of each other, were established by providence so that man may attain two goals. Undoubtedly neither the inseparability of the civil life from the religious nor the ideal superiority of the heavenly goal over the earthly could have escaped Dante; nor is it conceivable that so logical a mind as his could have neglected to consider how the emperor might reconcile the obedience owed to the pope in matters pertaining to the spiritual sphere with the independent exercise of his office. He must have thought that divine law, which clearly, in so many ways, declares itself in favor of the separation and independence of the two offices, was sufficient. For, if reverence on the part of the emperor is lacking in those matters

---
* *Ibid.*, III, xv, 7–10; *ibid.*, IV, xvi, 6–9.

where it is obligatory, does not the pope possess the God-given authority of a father to recall his son? And on the other hand, if greed for earthly things were to drive the pope to injustice and to appropriate what belongs to the other, would he not find a natural and legitimate check in the *executor iustitiae*?* One guide must serve as a curb to the other;† if not, let them both fear divine wrath.

Judge as you will the thought of Dante, this is the doctrine that appears in all his works. If in the *Monarchia* (an essentially political treatise) the author is more cautious in affirming the ideal subordination of the terrestrial to the celestial goal, he does not for all that deny it at the close of his essay.‡ In the poem, he scrutinizes it more openly. There he has in view not only the earthly but also the heavenly happiness of man. But whoever assigns so dominant a role, in the *Commedia*, to the emperor as to state that without imperial aid redemption would have no effect at all on eternal salvation, misunderstands the entire spirit of the poem. Dante certainly perceives the need of raising the Empire, once again, to a lofty station, in opposition to those who do not acknowledge it. He thinks that God will make use of a descendant of the Eagle to reëstablish order in the government of the world, since some extraordinary measure is necessary; but his idea is to institute the divine order no less in civil than in religious life. The Empire has no other task but that of aiding mankind to regain the perfection and the happiness of this world, a happiness once lost through original sin. Each authority has its proper place and its proper aim. If the world has wandered away from eternal salvation, it is not actually because it needs an emperor; it is because (and the poet strongly emphasizes

---
* *Mon.*, II, xi, 1.
† *Purg.*, XVI, 112.
‡ *Mon.*, III, xvi, 17–18.

it!) the spiritual guide misleads with his bad example, instead of showing the way toward good. If man does not reach his goal as an earthly creature, this happens through the fault of the papal usurper, because the Empire is hampered in its functions. And since the cure will be entrusted to the Greyhound or to the descendant of the Eagle, we must not confuse the ordinary role of the emperor with the special mission of the Messenger from heaven: he is to bring to an end the intrigue of the false shepherds with the tyrannical kings (only God knows by what means); but having accomplished his brief mission, he must then resume his proper role. Likewise the other guide, no longer blinded by greed for earthly things, will then take up again his high ministry and achieve what he alone is capable of accomplishing.

Present and Past in Dante's Vision

Convinced of the profound value of portraying the life of the other world as a means of saving this world from the pit into which it was about to plunge, Dante boldly attacked his subject. His vision embraced the entire history of mankind and the reality that pressed upon him on all sides. Alas, what a spectacle Florence made of herself, the "mighty city," the glorious daughter of Rome, so dear to his heart and so longingly yearned for during the years of bitter exile as the loveliest spot in the world,* the one in which he desired "with all his heart to rest his weary spirit" and to end his days.† Fratricidal wars robbed the city of every vestige of peace and of sweet communal existence; a perennial mutability of laws

---
* *De Vulg. Eloq.*, I, vi, 3.
† *Conv.*, I, iii, 4.

and proposals hindered all sure progress; her best citizens, who might have been able to supply Florence with good government, were downtrodden, oppressed, cast out. "Courtesy and valor" has disappeared; instead, "pride and excess" were flaunted by an upstart people who, having forsaken the countryside under the stimulus of a greedy desire for gain, had settled in town and overthrown all the virtues of civil and religious life. Italy, *nobilissima regio Europae*,* chosen by Providence to be the "garden of the Empire," with her people more inclined by nature than any other to rule the world because of her nobility and virtue,† she who was once mistress of provinces, was now a slave of passions and a hostel of woe. All Christianity, which had been redeemed at such a dear price from the abasement into which it had fallen, had ceased to care about the most precious gift of Faith and was being led astray by its rulers toward evil. Good kings were now but a memory and the ecclesiastical guides themselves gave the bad example of setting their hearts upon earthly goods. In this state of affairs, pondered again and again, suffered and deplored to no purpose, Dante's mind was carried toward two extremes: admiration for the past, sorrow and indignation about the present.

His judgment on his contemporaries is severe but impartial: he makes no distinction between this or that faction, this or that city in particular; he pours out his wrath equally on Guelphs and Ghibellines, friendly and hostile cities, the nobility and the upstarts. He feels only that he must strike hardest at those who are highest, those who, because of their position or office, have less excuse for error. His wrath becomes more violent in Paradise. The direct portrayal of turpitude and evil-doing in the other two canticles may be sufficient to con-

* *Mon.*, II, iii, 16.
† *Conv.*, IV, iv, 10.

demn the knighthood that defiles itself with usury, the noble families that practice common thievery, the palatine counts who become counterfeiters, the politicians who plunder cities; but the strongest reproaches against ecclesiastics are to be found only in heaven where everything is the expression of a righteous zeal.* In the third canticle we find the revelation of that which the blessed see in God; it is therefore natural that to them should be reserved the glorification or the condemnation of all that Dante most admired or detested. The corruption among the officials of the Church seemed to be the main cause for the degeneracy of the world, and Dante felt the duty of striking out at it, and he strikes. His anger, which pours forth with all the fury of which his great heart is capable, does not seem to be an outburst artificially induced, arising out of personal purposes or for a practical end, but rather a spontaneous and necessary product of his poetic invention.

Distaste for the present naturally leads to admiration of the past. His imagination therefore is continuously stimulated by the remembrance of it; it is kindled by the delineation and exaltation of those figures in the history of mankind who are most in conformity with the civil and religious ideals of his poetry. Such figures range from the great spirits of Limbo who, though alien to faith, are granted the grace of God because of their human virtues, and if not salvation, at least special honor, to the saints who worked most to keep religion in the purity of faith and the zeal of love, and were averse to worldly interests and empty knowledge. They range from Ripheus the Trojan who, still in the mire of paganism, loved justice alone and whose eyes therefore were open to future redemption by God, to Dante's fellow citizens of the preceding generation who, incapable of avoiding the weaknesses or

---

* *Par.*, XXII, 7–9.

THE DIVINE COMEDY 95

the arrogance of human nature, had at any rate turned their minds to good works for their commonalty and to the cultivation of those virtues that ennoble man. There was a time when examples of human virtues and of the perfect religious life were not far to seek. From that auspicious moment when, through divine will, at the approach of the redemption, "the ship of humanity sped over a gentle sea straight to its destined port,"* the good and well-governed world had lasted for centuries; and here and there, among new deflections of humanity, were oases of peace, virtuous ages on which a man might rest his eager glance. In distress, Dante compared the modern city with patriarchal Florence, still enclosed within the narrow compass of her most ancient walls, with her peaceful civic life, her pure and faithful, sober and virtuous population. He remembered that even in later days, notwithstanding factions and their battles for ascendancy, "courtesy and valor" ruled the city. In the minds of many there still lingered the memory of the flowering of these same virtues in the "land that is watered by the Adige and the Po"† and bounded "by the Po, the mountain, the seashore, and the Reno."‡

This era of peace and happiness which Rome had secured to the earth thanks to the two suns which had illumined the road of the world and the road of God, was it merely a dream of the poet? And had it been brought to an end by the donation of Constantine, or several centuries later? To be sure, the world suffered a great misfortune in that fatal donation; so great a misfortune indeed that humanity may be said to have been "destroyed" by it; but the effects were slow. According to Dante, the real downfall occurred no earlier than the thirteenth century when Frederick II had troubles with the

---
* *Conv.*, IV, v, 8.
† *Purg.*, XVI, 115.
‡ *Ibid.*, XIV, 92.

Church, when the theocracy of Innocent III, Gregory IX, and Innocent IV had put forth more assertive claims, and ecclesiastical law had become the chief occupation of the papal curia. Canon law was no longer kept within just bounds, that is, outside the province of the secular law, as in the time of Gratian. No longer were the Gospels, the councils, and the great doctors of the Church the foundation of Faith, the light and guide of the Church; their place had been usurped by the traditions *quas decretales dicunt.** These had the most fatal civil and religious results; for the Empire was so hindered in its functioning that men might call it "extinct," and no man cared any more for the sources of faith and the true interests of religion. Moreover, since the pastors were lost in vain knowledge, worldly honors, and the acquisition of material goods, the people, seeing their guides "striking out for the good which they covetously desire," also turned to greed. As a consequence, faith and justice had disappeared, and innocence and peace along with them.† The poet, of course, judges everything by the tribulations and hatreds which rack Florence and his Italy, and by the circumstances of so many unhappy Florentine exiles whose fate he shares. He voices a bitter pessimism that keeps him from perceiving so many signs of progress in his home city and in every other section of the peninsula as well as in neighboring countries.

It is a narrow vision, and partly untrue, but it is one into which the great heart of Dante pours all its feelings—a vision with which the most elevated poetry is amply suffused.

---

* *Mon.,* III, iii, 9-16; *Par.,* IX, 133-135.
† *Purg.,* XVI, 97-112; *Par.,* XXVII, 121-141.

Dante in His Poem

We will better understand this imaginative and emotional miracle if we fix our glance on the part that Dante plays in the poem. I do not refer to his role as prophet and seer, the result of the divine mission with which he feels himself invested, but to his role as a man who has a distinct personality and history of his own. This personality so pervades the poem that it may well be called a "Danteid." He is not Dante the sinner, as a certain school of criticism is wont to assert. He is lost, or so he believes. Once, he had been guided heavenwards to a life worthy of the outstanding qualities of his genius and mind; his guide was a chosen creature whom he thought sent by God. But now he seems to have lost all hope, even though all he has done or attempted to do has always been well-intentioned. He has committed no serious sin; nevertheless, in his "upright and pure conscience," in the eyes of the lady who has hastened to his aid from heaven, he realizes that he has not been able to guard against that taint and those worldly ambitions which are the sad heritage of humanity, even among those men who, according to the world, lived the most orderly domestic and civil life. Nor is this all he confesses. In his bitter contemplation of a world ruined by the unrestrained outbreak of passions, in the religious meditation to which he is compelled by the extraordinary privilege granted him of visiting the kingdoms of damnation and purification, in the exaltation of his spirit which ascends through the heavens filled with the glory of God—at such moments, of what value must the things of earth have appeared to him? Things to which he had given his time and care, which are esteemed most noble, like knowledge, or most necessary, like civil duties? In the poem we even find outbursts against these earthly concerns, outbursts which may seem confessions of sin, and we hear Beatrice reproaching him for having followed a philosophy alien to that of God. But all this is simply a reaction at certain moments, against worldly cares that oppress man and force him to discard higher aspirations. It is a just appraisal of two values of infinitely diverse rank. It is an ardent desire (and we have already pointed it out) for that eternal realm that he was depicting, compact of his imagination and his feelings. His desire is so intense that it impels him to condemn in its entirety this human life that is so different from the one he is contemplating. Actually he felt in himself no impurity that made him unworthy of Beatrice; and since the recognition of himself as a sinner (who can think of himself as pure before God?) does not discourage him from thinking that God may entrust him with so high a mission for the salvation of the world, those reactions, those momentary outbursts, do not lessen his admiration for all that man has been able to accomplish by virtue of the divine gift of reason. This is a basic idea in his mind and in the poem.

The complex personality of this man who is the center of so great a poetic vision is not easy to imagine. There is, in him, the true Christian, with that freedom of emotion and that sincerity which are characteristic of the age. There are no mystical outpourings, but God pervades the poem as the beginning and the end of all things, as a being present to all, as a good that most men have lost, to which many aspire, and in whom the elect rejoice. But we repeat: to be a Christian does not mean denying humanity; on the contrary, to be a Christian is to have a better understanding of the nobility of this divine creature, man, and the end for which God created him. That end is to achieve, through his own merit, as a soldier in the battles of the world, the glory of living eternally with Him. There is evil upon earth; it must be there, for without this danger, without this struggle, there is no reason for reward. The greatest gift that God has bestowed on man is free will, and it cannot be exercised without being continually exposed to risk; the more it is dragged by opposing forces toward evil, the more it will have the opportunity to display its mettle. Dante finds himself living in an age where everything is being hurled to perdition. We might call it a propitious moment for a heroic conscience. Dante, the man well versed in philosophy, the citizen resolute in doing good, is not only undismayed, but feels that he is able to show by example that in every situation man is the creator of his own destiny. He is convinced that perfection and happiness cannot exist except through the overcoming of all the obstacles that life places in our way. His moral conscience reacts, and fills with its vibrations whatever comes in contact with it, when he is confronted by the vision of evil that opposes him on all sides, when he has to cope with a world that his imagination impels him to create in order that it may mirror the fate of mankind. In how many destinies does he see reflections of his own feelings, his own misfortunes, his own ideals! How many characters afford him the opportunity to cast out of himself all that is unworthy, impure, unjust! How many opportunities for displaying his warm humanity and his piteous sympathy for the errors flowing from our nature even among the best and noblest sentiments! And with the most tender and gentle affections (like the love of family, dear friends, the fair brotherhood of art, feelings of gratitude, civic concord, and the like) are intermixed his love of learning, his admiration, we should say rather, his burning desire, for that ideal of man which streams from the civic life of past ages, gloriously revealed in the great figures of Limbo and in Cato, and which shines brightest in the saints who, with sublime morality, served the ends of their Creator.

Dante's Genius

It is difficult to determine the quality of Dante's genius. To proclaim him the "sovereign poet" or the hero of poetry, as is commonly done, is to speak of his greatness, but not of the nature of his genius. To call special attention to the adamantine temper of his character, his firm faith and strong will, the energy of his diction and the vigor of his style, is certainly to reveal one of the more notable aspects of his mind and poetry; but it is also to freeze him into an attitude as cold as his physical appearance in certain paintings. His inner life is more complex, richer, and his poetry more varied. Alongside the majestic and the powerful that bursts out of his strongest and most sublime conceptions, we find the simplicity, the freshness, the sweetness of a man who knows how to delineate the most fugitive aspects of nature, the most common occurrences of life, the most tender motions of the heart. Alongside this most refined artist, educated in the school of Virgil, (and, we must add, the good rhetorician too, developed in the medieval schools), we find the poet who contemplates, listens, and reproduces with native ingenuity, the directness and the boldness of the freest ages. So long as he deals with theories of art or with practical devices in application of the established tenets of the schools, the force of tradition works on his genius too, and we have, from time to time, assertions and artificial combinations that may make us smile today. All in all, however, there is displayed in him so deep a feeling for poetry as to enable him to understand and enjoy it independently of its exterior forms, in Latin as well as in the new vernacular. He evinces also a freedom of movement, in creating wholly beyond the fetters of any tradition, such as exists in few other geniuses of mankind. The same patient cultivation of art, together with the clarity and sense of proportion of the Latin genius, has been instrumental in giving a precise and harmonious portrayal of a world so remote from our imagination and so different from anything we have ever known as to seem miraculous. Even that which is pure artistic conceit, or that which is most reluctant to undergo a poetical transformation, finds vital and concrete expression by virtue of a happy combination of the most opposed gifts; so that what, by its nature, is most abstract and farthest from the reality of this world of ours, seems visible to our eyes. Dante succeeds in a thousand ways in giving the impression of having actually seen and heard what he relates and describes. Not only does he see, but he penetrates and chisels; with a few energetic strokes he knows how to reveal the soul of others in the look and attitude of the man himself, so that what that soul says and does seems natural and alive, as does that inward mystery that he does not trouble minutely to depict. Such is Dante's expressive power, that not only the reader who gives himself up to the free movement of the imagination, but even the student, endowed with awareness of the limits of his research, often becomes the victim of illusion and is prompted to raise questions on matters that are not expressed—as if one could create, through what is not clearly set forth, a genuine reality in matters of psychology, history, or topography.

Dante is predominantly a dramatic poet. If the scenes are rapid, this is so because of his energetic and concentrated conception, the result of his desire to find a means of displaying in his work all that fills his heart with so many needs, with so many memories, so many inclinations, and so many aspirations. But frequent, too, are the outbursts of his perturbed and embittered mind; so that harsh sketches of epic character are not lacking. A poem to which "both heaven and earth have set their hand," bursting out of a heart capable of the most diverse and profound responses, could not avoid presenting a great variety of inventiveness and tone. All the conditions and states of men and all the spectacles of nature, the events of the past and those of the present, that which most ennobles the spirit and that which most debases and lowers it; virtue and passion, truth and error, love and hate, joy and sadness, in all their most varied display, according to all customs and all ages—the whole of this is projected into a world which renders it more majestic and more suggestive. Nor is this poetry like a pageant of nature which reveals to, and awakens in, each of us those aspects and emotions to which we ourselves are most inclined. It is rather like a painting into which the soul of the painter has transfused a mighty emotion that increases many fold our powers of perception and response. The soul of Dante has entirely pervaded his work. It has given life to every idea offered to it by history and tradition. It has given new and deeper meaning to the things that surround us, and we are continually carried along by the intimate relationship that exists between the poet and his ideas. The fusion of so many disparate elements is perfect, because of the great intellectual effort Dante was able to sustain year after year, first in planning and then in composing his great poem. The fact that the descent of Henry was not enough to divert him from it, however great the anxiety with which he watched every new development and the impatience which every incertitude and every obstacle aroused in him, and the further fact that not even the ill-fortune attending the imperial expedition could break the drive of his inspiration, demonstrate the temper of his genius, and give us the reason for the power of his poetry. Just as his mind is mighty, varied, original, so is his art.

The true instinct of a poet and the natural impulse toward a new art are revealed in the choice of language. It is a language that is, first of all, living, and not the language of the schools and the tradition in which even Petrarch writes his *Africa;* moreover, it is not the language of the canzoni of love and virtue, so carefully sifted according to the scrupulous theories of the *De Vulgari Eloquentia,* but a richer language, which constituted for him a liberating medium, the instrument for a fuller, more varied, and more effective depiction of the world that whirled before his imagination. He knew how to find the language that suited his needs, with a happy contrivance of new methods and a wise choice of words appropriate to a poem that was to bestow individual and powerful form on all the emotions and illusions of which human nature is capable. It is no exaggeration to consider Dante the real creator of Italy's poetic and national language. Even if in our own more refined age, when poetic language has been more narrowly sifted, we come to the conclusion that his language is a little rough, somewhat unrestrained, we shall still have to recognize in it an unparalleled richness, a bold vigor. The very uncertainties of use and the strictures of rhyme have often given the poet the opportunity of avoiding worn-out expressions and of finding in the treasure of his imagination striking and mighty images that cause delight by reason of their very unexpectedness. The little touch of tartness, of the not too refined, has its place in a poem which, because of its infinite variety, cannot be evenly polished and smoothed throughout. The *Commedia* is like a juicy, savory fruit made more tasty by a certain pungency in its flavor.

The question has often arisen whether Dante may be considered a forerunner of the Renaissance. Here we must make a distinction. If by Renaissance is meant the rebirth of culture and art in the period which followed the darker centuries of the Middle Ages (the Revival, i.e., of an art and a culture which, while harking back to the ancients, was adjusted to new needs and new circumstances), he is more than a precursor; he is an initiator of it and one of its most outstanding masters. It is true that he did not effect innovations in philosophy and science, but rather repeated old things; however, even in these domains, he revealed a mind full of a purpose to see, to examine, to discuss, with an ardor and passion that even more learned men fail to evince. By breaking the prejudice that Latin was the only vehicle of philosophy and science, he heralded the vulgar tongue as the "new sun that will rise when the old one sets." In art, then, it was he who restored poetry to Italy; nay, he did not restore the poetry of Rome, but brought a new poetry in a new tongue, worthy of that old tongue; a poetry which no man afterwards was capable of surpassing.

If, instead, by Renaissance is meant the culture and spiritual life which existed in the fifteenth and sixteenth centuries, of course Dante is a man of an age two hundred years earlier. In certain respects he is still a medieval man, and we shall have to be content with placing him among the early forerunners of this traditional Renaissance. But what a forerunner! Above all, he was a layman, not a cleric. He may have attended the schools of the religious orders when the need for learning turned him to philosophy; he may have become a disciple of Albertus Magnus and Thomas Aquinas; he may have known Aristotle through the commentaries (what other means was available to him?). His earliest stimulations, nevertheless, came from Brunetto Latini, that is, from a school that prepared the citizen for civil life; from vernacular poetry, thought to be a complement of the gentleman's life and a necessary part of it for the practice of courtesy and valor; and, lastly, from Latin poetry. From the latter he received his artistic education, the value of which no one has ever better demonstrated; at the same time he learned from it a lesson in deep humanity and civic pride. Latin poetry was a glorification of Rome and the Empire, that is, of that city and government necessary for peace and justice among men. Dante's inner resources developed through participation in the active and exciting life of his city. If in exile he assumed duties, they were those of a "man of court" in the highest sense. When forced to meditation and writing because of his inability to serve in any other way, he fulfilled the duties of one who was born to follow "virtue and knowledge" and wanted to be useful to the commonwealth while leaving his reputation to posterity. His admiration for Athens "in which every branch of knowledge has its roots" even leads him to christen with her name the eternal city of heaven where every truth will be displayed;* and who has felt and glorified the fame of Rome as he has?

It is noteworthy, too, that no one has defended the separation of spiritual and civil power with greater zeal. Remote from all exaggerated asceticism, and loyal to the Italian religious mind, he does not condemn this earthly life for the future one, does not belittle the duties which it imposes, and the benefits which it brings. We have already noted how lively are his respect and the admiration for human virtue, even when they are to be found disassociated from faith. Even the virtues of the individual that were most in favor with the men of the Renaissance are fully developed in him. If he lags behind the Renaissance in certain things, in others he outdistances it and is freer: he esteems the poetry and admires the art of Virgil as well as that of the Psalms and the best troubadours; he recognizes the excellence of Latin, but prefers to achieve fame in the vernacular; and since the love of philosophy and art never impairs his religious convictions, so the glory of pagan Rome does not make him less appreciative of the glory of Christian Rome as well.

---
* *Conv.*, III, xiv, 15.

Italy produced this genius before the close of the Middle Ages. Through him the country that had been the last among the Latin nations to produce a literature of her own, in one stroke surpassed them all. Nor was he merely Italy's poetic glory. He was and remained for centuries the voice of her nobility and stormy fortunes. If, by reflecting the most universal interests of mankind and by drawing the most enduring emotions of our nature, Dante kindles the admiration of the world, for Italians he remains the highest symbol of their civilization and is regarded with just pride as the true national poet.

Part IV
The Reputation and Study of Dante

Dante's own age soon realized that he was a great poet. There is no doubt that the grammarians of his age recognized this, even if they did not have a distinct perception of what seems to us to be poetry, or were unable to evaluate it critically. The *Divina Commedia* would never have become so popular because of its learning or its allegory alone. The fascination of the mysterious world that he depicted; the anxious longing, never totally eradicated from the human mind, to know our eternal fate; the satisfaction of finding out, even if only through a poetic vision, the destiny of so many people who have played great roles in the history of the world; the general interest in problems of politics and religion current at that time, recorded and settled in the poem; the passion for scenes in which human nature passes through the most varied moods of grief, hope, and joy; all these attractions, made powerful by Dante's great art, and presented in the language common to all, must have made, and indeed did make, the *Commedia* a living and universally sought-after book. Thanks to Dante these matters "breathe new life into dead poesy" and revive reverence for the poets of antiquity. The interest and admiration that the poem aroused are attested not only by the praise written about it, but also, especially, by the great number of manuscripts that have survived. They are widely scattered. Many of them are written on beautiful parchment decorated with the richest miniatures and details; the popularity of the poem is confirmed by a number of glosses on the margins of the manuscripts, by the summaries of the three canticles in verse, by the variety of commentaries composed in the first decades after the death of the poet. Before fifty years had passed, the *Commedia* was being read publicly in some universities and even in the lesser schools along with the great Latin writers. "Dantist" had become a title of honor, and the teachers of literature who sought lectureships listed, as one of their claims to superiority, their ability to supply a commentary to Dante. Florence herself assigned to Giovanni Boccaccio the task of expounding the *Commedia* in one of the churches of the city. He had expended great pains in making a beautiful edition of the poetical works of Dante (*Vita Nuova,* canzoni, *Divina Commedia*), transcribing them several times with his own hand, and prefacing the edition with a solemn eulogy of its author.

Among the early epitomizers in verse we find Dante's son Iacopo, Messer Bosone da Gubbio, the Carmelite Guido da Pisa who added Latin notes to his compendium, Giovanni Boccaccio, Cecco di Meo degli Ugurgieri of Siena, and Mino di Vanni of Arezzo. Glosses were written on the first canticle either in Latin or the vernacular by Iacopo Alighieri, Ser Graziolo Bambaglioli, who was chancellor of the commune of Bologna, Guido da Pisa,[1] and by an anonymous Sienese who promises to continue his work through the *Purgatorio* and the *Paradiso*. Commentaries on the entire *Commedia* were written by Iacopo della Lana of Bologna probably during the 1320's, by an anonymous Florentine (the notary Andrea Lancia?) whose work was called *Ottimo* and who left three different editions of his notes, and by Pietro Alighieri, who also reworked his commentary no less than three times.[2]

When public lectures on the *Commedia* were inaugurated in the second half of the fourteenth century, more detailed and connected commentaries began to appear: first, that of Boccaccio (up to Canto XVII of the *Inferno*), second, that of Benvenuto Rambaldi da Imola, lecturer on Dante at Bologna, in several editions, and shortly after his, the commentary of the grammarian Francesco di Bartolo da Buti, who gave elucidations of the great poem in his school at Pisa. A good commentary on the entire *Inferno* and almost half the *Purgatorio* (the remainder being little more than a transcription from Iacopo della Lana) was left to us toward the end of the century by another anonymous Florentine, also a teacher of literature and a connoisseur of the classics as well as of the vernacular writers and of the life and history of Tuscany. But neither Dante's own sons nor the other admirers who set themselves to glossing and explaining the *Commedia* in the years closest to its composition seemed to have a precise knowledge of the poet's inner life or ideals, nor of the events and people about whom he writes. However, in succeeding centuries their work was of great importance for the study of the poem owing to the evidence they had collected from oral tradition, or from chronicles and other records that have not come down to us. They will continue to be important. Although they are to be used with critical caution, according to the age, the region, the culture, and the probable source from which they derive, they remain, after the minor works of Dante, the best aid to understanding the *Commedia*, the starting points for new research, and exceedingly valuable evidences of the linguistic usage of the times.

From the end of the fourteenth through the eighteenth century, Dante's reputation continued to grow, although it was a subject of continual debate owing to the changes in literary taste and in civilization itself and to the steadily increasing obscurement of the close relation which the *Commedia* bears to the culture and the spirit of the Middle Ages. In the period of humanism we find that enthusiasm for classical antiquity and the Latin language is an obstacle to the cult of Dante; then, in the sixteenth century, there comes to the fore that fastidious taste introduced into vernacular literature through the influence of Petrarch and his followers; in the following centuries we are confronted with the contempt of classical criticism for irregular literary forms and the disdain of the moderns for the ancients. In addition to being obscure, Dante is in bad taste: for those who most follow fashion he is, flatly, barbarous, or, as was said, "gothic"; he is praiseworthy only for certain episodes, for a few tercets where his genius succeeds in overcoming the bad taste of his age. But Florence remained faithful to her great poet and, in the fifteenth century, produced a learned commentator, Cristoforo Landino, who gathered together and edited the best of the ancient interpreters, and, in the sixteenth century, a group of defenders and expositors of Dante's work (Giovan Battista Gelli and Benedetto Varchi among others) who, if they did nothing else, managed to perpetuate the cult of Dante. The number of Dante admirers, lecturers, and students increased in other parts of Italy as the language of the three great Florentine poets became national; and the *Commedia* was among the first works to become widely known through the use of the printing press. If the commentaries of Friar Giovanni da Serravalle and Guiniforte Bargigi remained in obscurity before the invention of the press, certain others had a wide circulation: in addition to the commentaries of Lana and Landino, those published in Venice about the middle of the sixteenth century by Alessandro Vellutello and Bernardino Daniello of Lucca. Even the minor works began to appear in print, and from Venice in the eighteenth century came the first edition of the complete works. In this same century Father Pompeo Venturi and the Franciscan Friar Baldassarre Lombardi produced commentaries suited to the modern taste. Looking over these four centuries we find many serious students and admirers of Dante among writers who were not primarily concerned with him. Among them are Leonardo

Bruni of Arezzo, the defender of Dante against the exaggerations of the humanists and the author of a *Vita* based upon letters and documents which are no longer extant; Vincenzo Borghini, a great connoisseur of the history and language of ancient Florence, who was able to point out what had escaped the interpreters of his age and to deal judiciously with Dante's poetry; G. B. Vico, who, better than any other person up to that time, directed attention to the sources of the sublime in Dante; Gasparo Gozzi, who defended the poet against the strictures of Father Saverio Bettinelli, urged the interpreters to become "contemporaries of Dante" through study, and emphasized the value of the political thought in Dante's minor works for a complete understanding of the *Commedia:* and, last of all, Bartolomeo Perazzini of Verona who first brought sound principles of criticism to bear upon the correction of the text of the poem and gave great assistance to the labors of Lombardi and of that zealous Dante student, his compatriot, G. J. Dionisi.

In nineteenth-century Italy, the reputation and study of Dante became organized and spread to all the civilized world. The admiration of Alfieri, Parini, Monti, Foscolo, Leopardi for him was the first and most noteworthy sign of a great new movement in the life of that period and of its art, a movement which created a better climate for the understanding of Dante's profound poetry. "Dante padre" became the poet's common title; Balbo proclaimed him "the most Italian Italian there has ever been"; and from 1798, when at the first gleams of liberty the *Divina Commedia* was carried, crowned with the laurel, to the tomb in Ravenna and the poet publicly commemorated by Monti, to 1865, when in every part of Italy, *redenta* or *irredenta,* the sixth centenary of Dante's birth was celebrated as a national holiday, Dante became a symbol on the spiritual pennant of all patriotic and humanitarian ideals.

Mazzini writes: "That great spirit of his visualized Italy as the enduring initiator of religious and social unity in Europe and as an angel of civilization to the nations. The Italy he foresaw is the one we shall one day achieve." This idea may have led to some exaggeration or deflection in the study of Dante; but the interpretation of the *Commedia* broadened from narrowly moralistic and religious exegesis to a fuller understanding of the inspiring thought behind such great poetry; and the study of Dante, considered a duty, grew more and more intensive. Unfortunately, it lacked a sure and disciplined direction. The general historical movement helped indirectly, but not even Balbo and Troya were able to give to Dante that unflagging and unprejudiced attention which would have been necessary to reproduce the knowledge and thought of Dante's age as he depicted it in his work. Giosafatte Biagioli, Paolo Costa, Niccolò Tommaseo, Brunone Bianchi, Pietro Fraticelli, Raffaele Andreoli, and G. B. Giuliani were all commentators who better fulfilled the needs of their time; but their work was always superficial, and even Tommaseo seemed more concerned with comparisons, personal considerations, and digressions than with identifying himself with the poet.

Meanwhile, however, the extraordinary renascence of literature and art which occurred during the eighteenth and nineteenth centuries in Germany had led to great emphasis on the original work of geniuses of all epochs and countries; here Dante became the object of the most precise appraisals and the most intensive studies. There began in that country, from her interest in the art of all peoples, the flowering of Dante studies that culminated in the time of King John of Saxony (Philalethes), and that produced besides King John a group of noteworthy enthusiasts and Dante worshippers, such as

Karl Witte, F. C. Schlosser, L. G. Blanc, Karl Bartsch, Theodor Paur, Edward Böhmer, Emil Ruth, and F. S. Wegele. It was through Wegele that a branch of the Dante Society was founded at Dresden in 1865. This German movement made appreciable contributions to textual criticism and to the explication of Dante's works through the exploitation of the old commentaries and of the sources of Dante's learning. However, it gradually narrowed down to purely philological research, the investigation of particular questions of erudition and to minute exegesis; with Witte the interpretation of the *Commedia* became dominantly moral. These German researches had a zealous disseminator, although of less sound judgment, in the Swiss G. A. Scartazzini. Germany has continued, to the present day, to produce devoted and worthy students of Dante, such as Adolf Gaspary, F. S. Kraus, Alfred Bassermann, Karl Vossler, and others. Through them, that nation has greatly furthered the progress of Dante studies.

The example of Germany was followed by England where we find not only translations and works of popularization, Dante societies and Dante professorships, but also works of a scientific nature. Lord Vernon helped Witte to spread the knowledge of the ancient commentaries on the *Commedia* and of the text of the first editions; by his investigations H. C. Barlow aided textual criticism and the historical explanation of the poem. Their lead was followed in our day, with better results, by Edward Moore and Paget Toynbee. Competing with England is America, where Dante has had admirers of the caliber of Longfellow, James Russell Lowell, and Charles Eliot Norton. To the contributions of these must be added an intelligent and continuous work of popularization by means of translations, lectures, societies, and Dante collections. American scholars have directed their labors to the composition of works of scientific interest, such as concordances, catalogues, and bibliographies, which are most useful to Dante scholars all over the world.

Today, in no civilized nation does Dante lack admirers, but, with due exceptions, of course, works of assimilation and dissemination, rather than path-breaking researches, are contributed. Even in France this has generally been true.

In Italy, Dante studies took a more scientific turn during the second half of the nineteenth century. In the first half, Giuseppe Todeschini had already shown promise in historical and philological criticism; the simultaneous effort of Giosuè Carducci, Alessandro D'Ancona, Adolfo Bartoli, Isidoro Del Lungo, Francesco D'Ovidio, and Pio Rajna produced better results. At the same time, Francesco De Sanctis led criticism to examine the poet in Dante and to analyze his most beautiful creations in such a way as to see them with the same eyes as the author and to view them with the same emotions. Serious and conscientious workers were produced by this school, although their number is always less than that of pedants and improvisers. In 1888 a Dante Society was founded and it has had fruitful results. The criticism and interpretation of Dante gain constantly in breadth and subtlety.

Translator's Notes

NOTES TO PART I: THE LIFE OF DANTE ALIGHIERI

[1] A brief explanation here about the origin of the Guelph and Ghibelline parties should serve to clarify their traditional affiliations, respectively papal and imperial.

In the twelfth century the contenders for the crown of Germany were Conrad of Hohenstaufen and Henry, Duke of Bavaria and Saxony. Their quarrel culminated in the death of Henry, and the struggle was carried on in behalf of Henry's infant son by his uncle, Henry the Lion. At the siege of Weinsberg in 1140 the battle cries were for *Welf* or *Waiblingen* and these became party names: Welf, for the house of the Duke of Bavaria, and Waiblingen for Conrad of Hohenstaufen. (Waiblingen was the name of the Suabian castle and village where Conrad was born.) The Welfs were identified as the party of the great feudality, and the Waiblingen as the party of the monarch. These names were carried into Italy as *Guelph* and *Ghibelline* and came, generally speaking, to denote: one, the party of the papacy and Italian local independence of the emperor; and two, the imperialist party.

On the death of Conrad, the crown passed to his nephew Frederick I (Barbarossa) who, in 1154, entered Italy to seek the imperial crown. In Germany the political struggle between Frederick and Henry of Bavaria, Frederick's most powerful vassal, continued in sporadic outbreaks until Frederick partitioned the great duchy of Saxony in 1181. In the meantime many of the towns in Lombardy asserted their independence of both the feudal and episcopal governments. When the Emperor Henry VI died in 1197 the German crown was again the object of dispute; this time between Henry's brother Philip of Swabia and Otto, Duke of Bavaria, son of Henry the Lion. The emperor's son Frederick II was a child at this time. At length Philip of Swabia was successful in gaining the crown, but was shortly thereafter murdered. The next year, 1209, Otto of Bavaria gained the throne. In 1211 he was excommunicated by Pope Innocent III and Frederick II of Hohenstaufen was crowned king in 1215. Pope Innocent's command to the Italian cities to acknowledge Frederick met opposition, particularly in Florence. When Frederick II became emperor in 1220 he made it clear that he would uphold the independence of the imperial throne and was in consequence quickly denounced by the pope.

Frederick's supporters were the Ghibellines, nominally the party of the emperor, protector of the feudality. Frederick's opponents were the Guelph party, nominally, supporters of the pope, protector of the rights of the Italian communes.

These affiliations are thus conveniently definable, but it must be remembered that neither party served such clear-cut causes in the practical politics of the commune. They were, in the last analysis, local parties whose quarrel with each other often had nothing to do with the great struggle between the empire and the papacy. Their principal aim was control of the commune, and on their hope of assistance from pope or emperor depended the name of the party.

² Giovanni Villani, *Cronica,* VIII, 10.

³ Guinizelli, with a few poems, especially with the canzone "Al cor gentil," had provided samples of a new art better suited emotionally to the new ideals of the Italian people. (Barbi.)

⁴ The word used here by Barbi is *cavallata* which may be freely rendered "service of nobleman on horseback"; it refers to the traditional obligation of all men of means in the commune to maintain a horse to be used for military service in time of war. The cavalry was, of course, made up of those able to afford horses, namely, the nobles, but as time went on, many of the citizens upon whom the duty was laid were the newly rich burghers, the *popolani grassi,* who managed to evade their obligation by making a money payment. The old nobility, however, took pride in keeping up the tradition. For a brief description of the municipal army, see Ferdinand Schevill, *History of Florence,* pp. 194 ff.

⁵ Gemma was cousin to Corso Donati, but of a branch of the family that was soon to detach itself from the original stock by taking a new name. (Barbi)

⁶ "... After ... Charles II had succeeded to the kingdom of Naples, Florence gave a great reception to Charles II's son Charles Martel when he came, with a retinue of two hundred knights, to meet his father and mother there, and spent three weeks in the city. Dante was

in his twenty-ninth year, the recognized leader of the notable group of Florentine poets, ardent, romantic, public-spirited, confident. Charles, six years Dante's junior, already King of Hungary, heir to the Kingdom of Naples and the County of Provence, and son-in-law of the late Emperor Rudolph, handsome, musical, popular, was expected to take a great place in the world's affairs. Nothing is known but what is told us here of the personal relations between Charles and Dante; but the language of the canto is enough to prove a warmth of attachment which is in accord with all we know of both and from which we may guess something of Dante's grief for the death of the young prince from plague in the following year." John D. Sinclair, *The Divine Comedy of Dante Alighieri*, III, p. 129.

[7] For the sake of consistency, it is not to be believed that he belonged to the Council of the Podestà or to that of the commune during the second semester of 1295, and that he therefore had a part in the provisions favoring the magnates on July 6 of that year. (Barbi.)

[8] According to Dante's biographer, Leonard Bruni (1369-1444), the Whites were allowed to return from exile because of the illness of Guido Cavalcanti. Guido had contracted malaria during his exile and died as a result of it in August, 1300.

Although Guido is to be remembered as the close friend of Dante's early literary years, as the master of the subtle psychology of love expressed in the language of the *dolce stil nuovo*, and as the person to whom Dante dedicated the *Vita Nuova*, he is also to be remembered as the noble gentleman of Florence, the avowed enemy of Corso Donati who once attempted to assassinate him, and who himself in return attacked Corso on the streets of Florence.

[9] Dino Compagni, *Cronica*, I, xxii.

[10] *Ibid.*, I, xx.

[11] *Ibid.*, II, xi. The two men here named, Vieri de' Cerchi and Corso Donati, were the leaders respectively of the opposing factions in the Guelph party. Vieri was the richest banker of the day, head of a great trading company in Florence, and wielded a powerful influence among the lawyers and merchants of the guilds. His staunch opponent, Corso Donati, of a nobler but less wealthy lineage, was himself a leader among the magnates. On the issue of accepting the stringent provisions of the Ordinances, forced on the magnates in 1295, Vieri and Corso found themselves upholding opposing points of view. Vieri wished to yield

to the Ordinances; Corso was totally opposed. In Pope Boniface VIII, Corso found a champion, for Boniface planned to use Corso's faction to acquire control of Florence. The Jubilee of 1300 prevented the progress of this plan, but during the same year Boniface laid his plans with Charles of Valois who, before proceeding to the subjugation of Sicily, was to repair to Florence to put an end to the obstinacy of the Cerchi group.

The Cerchi, well aware of the danger in store for them, and fearful of their exposed position, should Florence lose her control over neighboring Pistoia, allied themselves with a group of Pistoiese called Whites, and helped them drive their opponents, a group called Blacks, from the city. The Blacks naturally called upon the Donati, and from this set of affiliations, the Cerchi with the Whites and the Donati with the Blacks of Pistoia, resulted the designations by which the two Florentine factions came to be known.

When, according to plan, the forces led by Charles of Valois came to Tuscany, the Whites, under the leadership of Vieri who now feared for his great investments, offered no resistance and Charles rode into the city unopposed. Corso, apparently with the support of Charles, came into the city from which he had been banished during Dante's priorate, and wreaked his vengeance upon his White enemies.

[11] Charles, Count of Valois, Alençon, and Anjou (1270–1325), was a son of Philip III, and brother of Philip IV, King of France. Pope Boniface had persuaded him to come to Italy to help his father-in-law Charles II of Anjou, King of Naples and Sicily, recover the island, which had been lost to the Angevin house by the revolt known as the Sicilian Vespers in 1282, from Frederick of Aragon.

[12] Although the fact of Dante's mission to Rome with Maso di Ruggierino and Corazza of Signa has been seriously questioned by scholars, the general tendency today is to accept Barbi's view that Dino's testimony is trustworthy. Leonardo Bruni and the author of the *Ottimo Commento*, together with Dino, assert that Dante was away at Rome when Charles of Valois entered Florence. Dino's terse account is worth repeating.

When the ambassadors arrived in Rome, the pope received them alone in his chamber, and said to them in secret, "Why are you so obstinate? Humble yourselves before me. And I say to you in truth that I have no intention but to bring about your peace. Let two of you

TRANSLATOR'S NOTES 121

go back, and let them have my blessing if they can cause my will to be obeyed." (Dino Compagni, *Cronica*, II, iv; see also II, xi, xxv.)

[14] Leonardo Bruni, *Vita di Dante*.

[15] Baldo d' Aguglione, Dino Compagni's "most wily lawyer," had been a prior in 1298 and again in 1311. In the latter year he drew up the decree that recalled many exiles but expressly excluded Dante's name. In 1299 he had been convicted of cutting out an inconvenient entry from one of the public records. Dante refers to him in the *Commedia* with great indignation: *Purg.*, XII, 105 and *Par.*, XVI, 56; see also Dino Compagni, *Cronica*, I, xix and II, xxx, for parts of Baldo's career.

[16] Robert of Naples, eldest son of King Charles II (Anjou), Duke of Calabria, on his father's death King of Apulia. Duke Robert was elected leader of the Blacks of Florence in the siege of Pistoia in 1305.

[17] On the amnesty of June 2, 1316, proclaimed by the Florentine magistrate, Lando of Gubbio, and the conditions imposed for recall from exile, we have Dante's comment in a letter to an unidentified friend: "... as to the decree recently passed in Florence concerning the pardon of the exiles: That if I will consent to pay a certain sum of money, and be willing to bear the brand of oblation, I may be absolved and may return at once. Wherein are two things ridiculous and ill-advised, O father! I say ill-advised by those who have expressed them; for your letter, more discreetly and advisedly drawn up, contained no hint of them.

"Is this the glorious recall whereby Dante Alighieri is summoned back to his fatherland after suffering well-nigh fifteen years of exile? Is this the reward of innocence manifest to all the world, of unbroken sweat and toil in study? Far be it from the familiar of philosophy, this abject self-abasement of a soul of clay! To allow himself to be presented at the altar, as a prisoner, after the fashion of some Ciolo or other infamous wretch. Far be it from the preacher of justice, when he hath suffered a wrong to pay his coin to them that inflicted it as though they had deserved well of him.

"Not this the way of return to my country, O my father! but if another may hereafter be found by you or any other, which hurts not Dante's fair fame and honor, that will I accept with no lagging feet. If no such path leads back to Florence, then will I never enter Florence more. What then? May I not gaze upon the mirror of the sun and stars wherever I may be? Can I not ponder on the sweetest truths wherever I may be beneath the heaven, but I must first make me inglorious, nay infamous, before the people and the state of Florence? Nor shall I lack for bread." (Epistle IX, *Latin Works*, trans. P. H. Wicksteed and A. G. F. Howell.)

[18] Uguccione della Faggiuola was a famed Ghibelline leader who became lord of Pisa shortly after Henry VII died in 1313. In the crisis that resulted in Florence as a result of the alarm that his power inspired, Florence issued a general recall of exiles, May 19, 1315, under the terms of a fine, a token imprisonment, and the ceremony of oblation. We know that Dante firmly rejected the conditions of return. It was this same year that saw the great rout of the Guelph armies by Uguccione at Montecatini, August 29, 1315. In the following year, Uguccione's power declined, and he was forced to go to Verona where Cangrande della Scala had become the great Ghibelline leader of northern Italy, and in his service Uguccione died, 1320.

[19] Taddeo Gaddi's portrait in fresco on the choir screen in Santa Croce, Florence, was destroyed in 1566. It is preserved more or less faithfully in a fifteenth-century miniature inserted before the text in the Codex Palatinus 320, a collection of Dante's lyrics, in the Biblioteca Nazionale, Florence. There is another portrait in the Eugenianus Codex, of the *Divina Commedia* in the Palatina, Vienna. A variant of the same type appears on a tempera panel of the fifteenth century in the collection of Prince Trivulzio, Milan. Another early fifteenth-century portrait is the colored frontispiece in the Codex Riccardianus in the Biblioteca Riccardiana, Florence. The frontispiece to our earlier cloth edition represents Dante, with the *Divina Commedia* in his left hand, standing before a gate in Florence, the mount of Purgatory in the background, the portal of Hell at his right, and the circles of Paradise traced in the sky. This is a tempera panel by Domenico di Michelino in Santa Maria del Fiore, Florence. One of the best known representations of the poet is the colored plaster bust by an unknown sculptor, in the Uffizi Gallery, Florence; this is known as the Torrigiani "death mask," and was presented to the Uffizi in 1840 by Marchese Pietro Torregiani. Probably the best known of all representations of Dante is the famous bronze bust in the Farnese Collection in the Museo Nazionale, Naples. This bust was probably the work of a Florentine imitator of Donatello in the sixteenth century. It agrees closely in facial

proportions and in other features with the portrait in the Codex Palatinus. There are two interesting portraits on fifteenth-century wooden chests (*cassone*); one, painted by Giovanni dal Ponte about 1440, and now in the Fogg Museum, Harvard University; the other, painted by Francesco Pesellino, about 1450, in the collection of Mrs. John L. Garner, Boston, Massachusetts.

NOTES TO PART II: THE MINOR WORKS

[1] A word of explanation is appropriate here. In this period the vernacular of southern France (the *langue d'oc*) is distinguished by the use of *oc*, "yes"; in the area of the Loire basin and in northern France (the *langue d'oïl*) by the use of *oïl*, "yes"; in Italy the vernacular (the *langue de sì*) uses *sì*, "yes."

[2] "O, if in happier times you should behold,
Mirrored amid your spring your silver hairs,
Adorned by Phillis' self, your sacred hairs
Turning again to fair, with what a strange
And sudden rapture would you feel anew
The coolness of your thickly spreading vine."

(Translated by Wilmon Brewer, *Dante's Eclogues*, p. 19)

NOTE TO PART III: THE DIVINE COMEDY

[1] See P. H. Wicksteed and E. G. Gardner, *Dante and Giovanni del Virgilio*, pp. 227–228 for a critical note on the Latin text.

NOTES TO PART IV: THE REPUTATION AND STUDY OF DANTE

[1] This second work of his still remains for the most part unpublished. (Barbi.)

[2] The so-called Cassino annotations are but literal transcriptions of his notes. (Barbi.)

Bibliographical Note

The following bibliographical note is not intended to provide a list of highly specialized, scholarly works on Dante. Those who wish this kind of bibliography may consult T. W. Koch's *Catalogue of the Dante Collection presented by W. Fiske to Cornell University* (2 vols., Ithaca, N.Y., 1898–1900), and M. Fowler's volume of *Additions, 1898–1920* (Ithaca, 1921). Smaller, but no less impressive in scope is the general bibliographical note on the Middle Ages appended to Karl Vossler's *Mediaeval Culture* (trans. W. C. Lawton, New York, 1929), compiled by J. E. Spingarn; and that specialized list of books, articles and monographs which forms the last section of Michele Barbi's article on Dante in the *Enciclopedia Italiana*, compiled for those expert in at least Italian and English.

All the books included here have a collective value that will put a more complete understanding of Dante, his times and his work within reach of students of literature who cannot read Dante in either his native Italian or Latin, but who wish nevertheless to acquaint themselves with his subject matter.

Translations of the *Divine Comedy* are of course too many to list here, but a word about the most available ones may be of assistance: H. F. Cary's blank verse rendering (London, 1814) still occupies a place of importance because of its remarkable vigor; H. W. Longfellow's version (3 vols., Boston, 1867–1871), also in blank verse, will satisfy those who are looking for a literal transcription of Dante's great poem. E. H. Plumptre's translation, *Commedia and Canzoniere* (2 vols., London, 1886–1887), is in Dante's original "terza rima," as is Laurence Binyon's *Divine Comedy*, now reprinted with C. H. Grandgent's notes in Paolo Milano's anthology of Dante for the Viking Portable Library (New York, 1947); J. B. Fletcher's translation, illustrated in the de luxe edition with the Botticelli sketches (New York, 1931), employs a modification of the "terza rima." Of approximately equal value among prose versions are the Carlyle-Wicksteed translation, available both in Temple Classics (3 vols., London, 1899–1900) and in the Modern Library edition (New York, 1932), that by C. E. Norton (3 vols., Boston, 1891–1892), and the recent very readable version with commentary by J. D. Sinclair (3 vols., London, 1940–1946).

The *Vita Nuova* has been elegantly translated by Dante Gabriel Rossetti in *Dante and His Circle* (London, 1864), and has been many times reprinted, most recently in *The Portable Dante* (see above); other literal versions are the ones by C. E. Norton (Boston, 1867), and by T. Okey for the Temple Classics (London, 1906). Charles Singleton's *An Essay on the Vita Nuova* (Harvard University Press, 1949), will prove both provocative and illuminating for the meaning of this early work as a whole.

The *Canzoniere* is available in Wicksteed's translation for Temple Classics (London, 1906), in Plumptre's above-mentioned *Commedia and Canzoniere*, and in Lorna de'Lucchi's *The Minor Poems of Dante* (Oxford, 1926).

The *Convivio* has been translated by E. P. Sayer, *Il Convito, the Banquet of Dante Alighieri* (London, 1887), by Katherine Hillard, *The Banquet of Dante Alighieri* (London, 1889), and by Wicksteed for the Temple Classics (London, 1904).

The complete *Latin Works* are printed in one volume of the Temple Classics (London, 1904), the work of P. H. Wicksteed and A. G. F. Howell. Howell's version of the *De Vulgari Eloquentia* for this edition is a revision of an earlier translation made in 1890; in connection with it the student should consult George Saintsbury's *History of Criticism* (vol. 2) for a penetrating and illuminating analysis of this work. Among other translations, the *De Monarchia* is available in Aurelia Henry's translation (Boston and New York, 1904), and in that of F. C. Church, printed in R. W. Church's *Dante, An Essay* (London, 1879); the *Letters* have been translated by C. S. Latham (Boston and New York, 1892), and by Paget Toynbee (Oxford, 1920); the *Eclogues* may be found with Latin text in *Dante and Giovanni del Virgilio* (Westminster, 1902), by P. H. Wicksteed and E. G. Gardner, and more recently W. Brewer has made a blank verse translation of them (Boston, 1927); the *Quaestio de Aqua et Terra* may be had in the version by A. C. White (Boston, 1903) and that by C. L. Shadwell (Oxford, 1909).

The two standard, one-volume editions of Dante's complete works are the "Oxford Dante," *Tutte le Opere di Dante Alighieri*, ed. E. Moore (4th ed., rev. by P. Toynbee, Oxford, 1924), and the Italian edition, *Le Opere di Dante*, ed. Michele Barbi and others (Florence, 1921).

E. A. Fay has compiled the *Concordance of the Divine Comedy* (London, 1894); E. S. Sheldon and A. C. White, the concordance to the other works in Italian (*Concordanza delle Opere italiane in Prosa e del Canzoniere di Dante Alighieri*, Oxford, 1905); and E. K. Rand and

E. H. Wilkins, the concordance to the Latin works (*Dantis Alagherii operum latinorum concordantiae,* Oxford, 1912). P. Toynbee's *Dictionary of Proper Names and Notable Matters in the Works of Dante* (Oxford, 1898), and the revised, condensed *Concise Dictionary* (Oxford, 1914) are mines of information. C. A. Dinsmore's *Aids to the Study of Dante* (Boston and New York, 1903) seems still to be a most useful book to use with either of the Toynbee dictionaries, and may well be the essential "other book" for the newcomer to Dante. E. G. Gardner's *Dante* (new ed., London, 1923) contains a convenient summary of each of Dante's works, with much other important information about his life, as also Toynbee's *Dante Alighieri: His Life and Work* (4th ed., London, 1910). Those who have made some progress in the reading of Dante will find Umberto Cosmo's *Handbook to Dante Studies,* trans. David Moore (New York, Barnes and Noble, Inc., n.d.), indispensable for its summary of the various problems associated with the poet's history and work. For portraits and iconography, R. T. Holbrook's well-illustrated *Portraits of Dante from Giotto to Raffael* (London, 1911), and F. J. Mather's *The Portraits of Dante Compared with Measurements of His Skull and Reclassified* (Princeton, 1921), may be profitably examined.

An extensive set of commentaries on the *Divine Comedy,* relatively free of moralizing, is that of J. S. Carroll, *Exiles of Eternity* [Inferno] *Prisoners of Hope* [Purgatorio], and *In Patria* [Paradiso] (London, 1904–1911); the comment which follows each canto in the translation by J. D. Sinclair (see above) is more concise and more objective. For both structure and ethical plan, H. W. V. Reade's *Moral System of Dante's Inferno* (Oxford, 1909) and E. G. Moore's two chapters, "Classification of Sins in the 'Inferno' and 'Purgatorio,'" and "The Unity and Symmetry of Design in the 'Purgatorio'" in *Studies in Dante* (vol. 2, Oxford, 1899) may be consulted. E. G. Gardner's *Dante's Ten Heavens* (Westminster, 1900) is an especially good guide through the third canticle.

The chief works dealing with Dante's influence upon English Literature are Paget Toynbee's *Dante in English Literature from Chaucer to Cary,* 1380–1844 (London, 1909) and *Britain's Tribute to Dante in Literature and Art* (London, 1921); with these, O. Kuhn's slight survey, *Dante and the English Poets from Chaucer to Tennyson* (New York, 1904), may be consulted. A. La Piana's *Dante's American Pilgrimage; A Historical Survey of Dante Studies in the United States,* 1800–1944 (New Haven, 1948) is a most welcome and needed account of the extent of Dante's cult in the United States. Equally welcome and needed is the great work by Werner Paul Friedrich, *Dante's Fame*

Abroad, 1350–1850; the Influence of Dante Alighieri on the Poets and Scholars of Spain, France, England, Germany, Switzerland, and the United States. A Survey of the Present State of Scholarship (Rome, Edizioni de Storia e Letteratura, 1950).

No one should overlook the early biographies of Dante by Boccaccio and Leonardo Bruni, both of which have been translated by P. H. Wicksteed for the King's Classics (London, 1904), and by J. H. Smith (New York, 1901). E. Moore's *Dante and His Early Biographers* (London, 1890) collates much of this primary material.

No modern account of Dante's age can match the fire of Dino Compagni's *Chronicle,* translated for Temple Classics by E. C. M. Benecke and A. G. F. Howell. Dino covers the period between 1280 and 1312, relating step by step the division of the Guelf party of Florence into the White and Black factions and the gradual control of the government of the city by the wealthy traders who were organized into the greater guilds. Dino's testimony may be compared with the more dispassionate story told by Giovanni Villani in R. E. Selfe and P. H. Wicksteed's *Selections from the First Nine Books of the Croniche Fiorentine of Giovanni Villani* (New York, 1907). P. Villari's *The First Two Centuries of Florentine History* translated by Linda Villari (2 vols., New York, 1894–1895), E. G. Gardner's *Story of Florence* (London, 1901), an account of the development of the city, and the first fifteen chapters of Ferdinand Schevill's *History of Florence from the Founding of the City through the Renaissance* (New York, 1936) will acquaint the reader with the story of the Florentine commune through the time of Dante. More general accounts of medieval Italy, like Karl Federn's *Dante and his Time* (New York, 1902), L. Ragg's *Dante and his Italy* (London and New York, 1907), P. Villari's *Mediaeval Italy from Charlemagne to Henry VII,* translated by Costanza Hulton (London and New York, 1910), H. D. Sedgwick, *Italy in the Thirteenth Century* (2 vols., Boston, 1912), and J. J. Walsh's *The Thirteenth, Greatest of Centuries* (New York, 1913), may all be used, with reservations.

No study of Dante would be satisfactory without a consideration of the reputation of Virgil in the Middle Ages. W. Y. Sellar's *Virgil* (Oxford, 1897), with its evaluation of the Roman poet in his own age, may be followed up with D. Comparetti's *Vergil in the Middle Ages,* translated by E. F. M. Benecke (London and New York, 1895), and with J. W. Spargo's *Virgil the Necromancer; Studies in Virgilian Legends* (Cambridge, Mass., 1934).

Boethius' *Consolation of Philosophy,* in the translation by E. K. Rand and H. F. Stewart for the Loeb Classical Library (London and New York, 1918), or in that of W. V. Cooper now available in the

Modern Library series (New York, 1943) is one of Dante's acknowledged sources, and should prove interesting from the point of view of the literary type as well as from that of subject matter. Additional information may be had concerning the life and times of Boethius in H. F. Stewart's old, but still stimulating *Boethius, An Essay* (Edinburgh and London, 1891); H. R. Patch's *The Tradition of Boethius; A Study of His Importance in Medieval Culture* (Oxford University Press, 1935); and in H. M. Barrett's *Boethius: Some Aspects of His Times and Works* (Cambridge, 1940). On the notions of Fate and Fortune, V. Ciòffari's *The Conception of Fortune and Fate in the Works of Dante* (Dante Society of Cambridge, Mass., 1940) is a scholarly monograph; H. R. Patch's *The Goddess Fortuna in Mediaeval Literature* (Cambridge, Mass., 1927) is a general treatment, both readable and interesting.

Dante's indebtedness to St. Thomas Aquinas is amply discussed in P. H. Wicksteed's *Dante and Aquinas* (London and Toronto, 1913); the thought of this great thinker may be studied at first hand in the translations made by the English Dominican Fathers, in the abridgment of the *Summa Contra Gentiles, Of God and His Creatures* by J. Rickaby (London, 1906), or in the *Basic Writings of Saint Thomas Aquinas* (New York, Random House, 1945) edited by A. C. Pegis. The volume *Essays in Thomism* (New York, 1942), edited by R. E. Brennan, contains among others chapters entitled "The Economic Philosophy of Aquinas," by A. Ryan, and "The Fate of Representative Government," by W. Farrell, both of which may serve to indicate the range of Thomistic thought. The ambitious may want to read Etienne Gilson's *Philosophy of St. Thomas Aquinas*, trans. E. Bullough (Cambridge, 1924), and then Gilson's *Spirit of Mediaeval Philosophy*, trans. A. H. C. Downes (New York, 1940), a book which defines Christian thought of the Middle Ages better than any I know. F. Ozanam's *Dante and Catholic Philosophy in the Thirteenth Century*, trans. D. Pychowski (New York, 1897), is still of value and deals actually with more than Dante's debt to scholastic philosophers. A convenient account is D. J. Kennedy's article, "Thomas Aquinas," in the *Catholic Encyclopedia*.

For translations of various hymns which are referred to in the *Divine Comedy*, Matthew Britt's *The Hymns of the Breviary and Missal* (rev. ed., New York, 1936) may be consulted, and W. O. E. Oesterly's *Jewish Background of the Christian Liturgy* (Oxford, 1925), A. Fortescue's *The Mass: A Study of the Roman Liturgy* (London, 1912), and his articles on "Liturgy," "Rites," "Canon of the Mass," and the like, in the *Catholic Encyclopedia* will satisfy questions in that direction.

J. H. Smith's *The Troubadours at Home* (2 vols., New York, 1899) is an extensive and enthusiastic treatment of the poetry of Provence; it contains many translations. Other translations may be found in Barbara Smythe's *Trobador Poets* (London, 1911) which contains poems of Arnaut Daniel and Bertran de Born; H. J. Chaytor's *The Troubadours* (Cambridge, 1912) is an elementary but convenient sketch of the whole movement. For accounts of each of the troubadour poets mentioned by Dante, Toynbee's *Dante Dictionary* is the readiest source. For the theory of love which underlies this body of poetry, L. F. Mott's slight *The System of Courtly Love Studied as an Introduction to the Vita Nuova of Dante* (Boston and London, 1896), W. A. Neilson's *Origins and Sources of the Court of Love* (Boston, 1899), and T. A. Kirby's *Chaucer's Troilus; A Study in Courtly Love* (Louisiana State University Press, 1940) are all of value, but the subject may best be approached through Andrew the Chaplain's *Art of Courtly Love,* trans. J. J. Parry (New York, 1941).

On the subject of allegory, the second chapter of C. S. Lewis' *Allegory of Love; A Study in Medieval Tradition* (London, 1936), J. Geffcken's article, "Allegory, allegorical interpretation," in Hastings' *Encyclopaedia of Religion and Ethics,* and J. A. Stewart's important remarks on allegory in *Myths of Plato* (London and New York, 1905) are all very informative; but Dante's own letter to Cangrande della Scala and *Convivio,* II, 1, will best supply the method.

Among histories of Italian literature A. Gaspàry's *History of Early Italian Literature to the Death of Dante,* trans. H. Oelsner (London, 1901), and F. De Sanctis' *History of Italian Literature,* trans, by J. Redfern (New York, 1931), are especially to be recommended for their sure manipulation of the many facets of medieval literary influences. For translations from individual poets, Rossetti's *Dante and His Circle* still stands foremost. Ezra Pound's versions of the poems of Guido Cavalcanti (Boston, 1912) are a satisfactory transcription of the sentiments of the school of poetry to which he and Dante belonged; Evelyn Underhill's *Jacopone da Todi: A Spiritual Biography* (London, 1919) gives both the Italian text and English translation of some of the Franciscan's lauds. Should the reader's interest lead him from this body of poetry to the Latin literature of the period and earlier, he may consult Matthew Britt for hymns (see above), and F. J. E. Raby's two works, *A History of Christian-Latin Poetry from the Beginnings to the Close of the Middle Ages* (Oxford, 1927), and *A History of Secular Latin Poetry in the Middle Ages* (Oxford, 1934), both of them more than ordinarily interesting accounts. He will wish, at any rate, to consult the fundamental essay by E. Moore, "Scripture and Classical Authors in Dante," in *Studies in Dante* (vol. I), on the extent of Dante's indebtedness to the Bible and to the writers of pagan antiquity.

E. C. Butler's article, "Monasticism," in the *Cambridge Mediaeval History*, volume 1 still seems to be the best starting place for a study of that important movement in Western civilization, and may be followed with Montalembert's fervid *Monks of the West from St. Benedict to St. Bernard* (6 vols., London, 1896). The *Rule of St. Benedict* may be read in a number of translations; the spirit of the followers of Benedict is nicely treated in Butler's *Benedictine Monachism* (London, 1919). G. G. Coulton's *Five Centuries of Religion* (vols. 1 and 2, Cambridge, 1927–1929), although valuable for the economic and social side of monasticism, is often otherwise sharply hostile.

Among the important figures mentioned in the *Divine Comedy* are St. Francis and St. Dominic, for which see J. Herkless, *Francis and Dominic* (London, 1901) and Coulton, *Five Centuries of Religion*, vol. 2, the article by M. Bihl on the "Friars Minor," and that by P. Mandonnet on the "Order of Preachers," in the *Catholic Encyclopaedia*, all of which deal with the rise of the Franciscan and Dominican orders; with these two articles may be consulted two others in the same work: M. Heimbucher's "Hermits of St. Augustine," and B. Zimmerman's "Carmelite Order," which are as good introductions to the four Mendicant Orders as can be found. The *Little Flowers of St. Francis*, translated by T. W. Arnold, is available in Temple Classics (London, 1903) as is E. Gurney-Salter's translation of *The Legend of Saint Francis by the Three Companions* (London, 1902). St. Bonaventure's *Life of St. Francis*, together with the *Mirror of Perfection* and the *Little Flowers of St. Francis* are available in the Everyman's Library (London, 1910).

The many stories about the saints circulated in Dante's time may be most conveniently read in the famous *Golden Legend* of Jacopus de Voragine, Dante's contemporary. This collection of lives, thought to be one of the books indispensable for a complete understanding of the Middle Ages, has been published by Temple Classics (7 vols., London, 1900) in Caxton's translation. G. Ryan and H. Ripperger have made translations and adaptations for a recent edition, *The Golden Legend of Jacobus de Voragine* (London and New York, 1941).

In the realm of medieval science, vast amounts of material may be found in George Sarton's *Introduction to the History of Science* (3 vols., Baltimore, 1927–1948), the last volume of which extends through the fourteenth century. Lynn Thorndyke's *History of Magic and Experimental Sciences in the First Thirteen Centuries of Our Era* (2 vols., New York, 1923) is especially good for bibliographies of the various sciences. C. L. Beazley's *Dawn of Modern Geography* (3 vols., London, 1897–1906), L. O. Wedel's *Mediaeval Attitude toward Astrology* (New Haven, Conn., 1920), and M. M. P. Muir's *Story of Alchemy and the Beginnings of Chemistry* (London, 1902) deal with individual sciences. E. Moore's *Studies in Dante* (vol. 3) contains chapters on Dante's use of astronomy and geography; R. T. Holbrook's *Dante and the Animal Kingdom* (New York, 1903), M. A. Orr Evershed's *Dante and the Early Astronomers* (London, 1913), and O. Kuhn's *Treatment of Nature in Dante's 'Divina Commedia'* (London, 1897) all deal with Dante's acute observation and long study of the objective world.

The great work on political theory for the Middle Ages is R. W. and A. J. Carlyle's *History of Mediaeval Political Theory in the West* (6 vols., Edinburgh and London, 1903–1936), but surveys like W. A. Dunning's *History of Political Theories, Ancient and Mediaeval* (New York, 1902), or G. H. Sabine's *A History of Political Theory* (New York, 1937) are perhaps more suitable for the purposes of this note; these surveys include discussions of the political theory of St. Thomas Aquinas and that of his disciple Egidio Colonna. As for Dante's own theory and its sources, W. H. V. Reade's essay, "The Political Theory of Dante," in the reprint of the Oxford text of the *De Monarchia* (Oxford, 1916), contains a good discussion of the poet's beliefs.

www.ingramcontent.com/pod-product-compliance
Lightning Source LLC
Chambersburg PA
CBHW021713230426
43668CB00008B/818